RING OF DOWNS

RING OF DOWNS

The North Downs' Eastern Ring

MARYANNE GRANT TRAYLEN

Leaf Light Publications

CONTENTS

A Song of the Rolling Earth Walt Whitman

Were you thinking that those were the words, those upright lines?
those curves, angles, dots?
No, those are not the words, the substantial words are in
the ground and sea,
They are in the air, they are in you.

... I swear the earth shall surely be complete to him or her who shall be complete.

An extract from *Ring of Downs* first appeared in the online journal *The Clearing*, Little Toller Books, 2020.

~ 1 ~

INTRODUCTION

Ring of Downs as sequel to *A Dog on the Downs* is a meditation, both verbal and visual, on what I call the North Downs' Eastern Ring. It is a peregrination, a walk with the dog, a symbiosis of word and image. What I have called the Eastern Ring is roughly the area stretching from Boughton Lees/Aluph in an arc leading northeast through Canterbury to Dover, and south-east in another lower arc through the Folkestone Downs to Dover. It opens up a relatively undocumented part of the North Downs and is also an imaginative response to the landscape, urging us to embrace a little piece of what surrounds us as our own more sensitively.

To become interested in this 'ring' topographically is also to become interested in it metaphorically. It became my mandala, mapping out all those varying shades, colours and moods that make up the whole person and their environment, the Self towards which we journey without arrival, imprinted here, upon the landscape. The present threat to nature challenges each of us to seek out our own mandala of place, so by restoring what is whole in us through a two-way process with nature, we begin to redress an imbalance caused by the plundering of our earth.z

Obligingly for my mandala metaphor – a design which brings together two halves – these two distinct arcs on the North Downs' Way eastern part are also brought together in this ring of which I have imagined the top leading through Canterbury to represent 'the way of the spirit'. The lower, 'the way of the flesh'.

Walking itself is also a tool for bridging this gap between mind and body, walking 'out to walk in', using action to achieve non-action, forging what walker and author Nan Shepherd describes as the 'thinking body'. Harnessing ourselves to the topography of place in unison with body, walking can reflect life's vicissitudes too, to be stomped in, out and through.Tucking my intuitive feather into the ribbon of my thinking cap, and with a desire to share some of the beautiful places I've discovered with others, I'm dividing this book to accommodate the mandala plan.

The first part covers a section of the straight area of the North Downs that leads along the Pilgrims Ways from Farnham. It begins for me at Lenham and leads through Charing, Westwell and Eastwell until it reaches the beginning of my Eastern Ring at Boughton Lees/ Aluph where the North Downs Way divides.

The next section shows the lower part of the circle or arc, after the Way's division, as it passes through Wye, Brabourne, Postling, Tolsford Hill, Etchinghill escarpment, Summerhouse Hill, the Arpinge escarpment, Peene quarry, the Folkestone Downs (Cheriton Down, Cherry Tree Hill, Castle Hill, Round Hill, Sugar Loaf Hill, Wingate Hill, Creteway Down, Dover Hill) until it reaches the white chalk cliffs at Folkestone then passes through Capel and Samphire Hoe to Dover.

The upper part of the arc travels northeast through King's Woods, Chilham, Chartham, Canterbury, Bekesbourne, Bishopsbourne, Shepherdswell to Dover. There is also be a section on the dry valleys, Elham, Lydden and Alkham (ELA) and the Saxon Shoreline overlooking Romney's marshes.

The two paths arching northeast and southeast from Boughton Aluph may not form a strictly circular mandala, but a rotundum nevertheless which forms an imperfect ring-like continuum. A baroque pearl it has been suggested, with nodules. Or the cross section of a cabbage or tree trunk which viewed imaginatively reveals beauty to lie in its imperfection.

The word 'mandala' comes from the Sanskrit meaning circle and was for Jung the most important 'uniting' symbol of the unknowable Self (Jung, 1963). Its patterns draw us towards the centre of our psyche, our identity and wholeness, like the drive of the seed towards its plant, the bud its flower (Harvest, 1997: 89). Jung's centripetal aspect of the Self shared something with the Tao principal that in nature everything reverts to its original root. The principal of circularity or returning saw that all things emanating from Tao would ultimately return there. (Harvest, 1997: 97): *Thereis no linear evolution, only circumambulation of the Self* (Jung, 1963: 222). The mandala as a shape, a pattern, a drawing or a dream arising spontaneously from the unconscious best expresses this circular rather than linear evolution of the Self. Engaging with nature is the means by which we can dissipate the Self and by 'unselfing' gain ourselves.

Making place special by relationship with it is a part of the journey. It imbues a scene with the numinous, that is something of the divine or spiritual, and makes pathways not always marked on the map, links walking with the imagination and sees the country we move through and shape, as shaping us in a two-way process. Perhaps landscape is a thinking and feeling sentient being too: a conduit to older thread-weaving mysteries that draw us in through time.

Of the place, Folkestone, from where I conduct my forays and researches, *Lapis Tituli*, 'inscribed stone', is the name once given to it. And of my companion, Dog, who I walk with, and who features as the visual constant in my photographs, is the one who becomes the rippling embodiment of imaginative thought, going out before me, streaking, sniffing, dipping and rising, black over green, white and blue.

As a 'meandering journey' and a 'meditation' this book is no guide or mapped-out walk manual about hiking, rather an exercise in how landscape impinged upon by our imaginations is elevated as a source of wonder, beauty and reflection. Like a spring from which we might draw strength to foster physical and mental wellbeing. A 'lung' through which to take a deeper breath.

In Lao Tzu and Jungian style I have allowed images to arise spontaneously, unreflectively, but also I have reflected. For in gleaning thoughts and feelings from the landscape to form the pattern of my mandala, I have focused on shapes to make them more consciously visible, laying pictures out on pages and editing words.

My intention is not to write about nature as if I were observer, for I am looking out to look in, and vice versa; writing and colouring the landscape with emotion, either in the tone of fauvism's 'wild beast' or with gentler greens of hills, and whites and blues of water falling.

Then again although this book is no guide, nor is it fiction, rather an imaginative in-depth exploration and interpretation of the paradox of what is there: the *particular* landmarks upon these Downs' 'ring' that make the *universal* distinct as an expressive symbol of individual Self, each of us finding our own mandala in landscape. Engaging with nature the means by which we can dissipate the Self and by 'unselfing' gain ourselves!

Harvest, Journal for Jungian Studies, 1997 Vol 43 No 2, C.G.Jung APC, London, p 86, fds *Jung and Taoism, A Comparative Analysis of Jung's Psychology and Taoist Philosophy*, Khong, Belinda, SL and Thompson, Norman L.

Jung, C.G. 1963, *Memories, Dreams and Reflections*, ed. Jaffe, London, Flamingo

Jung, C.G. (1973). *Experimental Researches,* Collected Works of C.G. Jung, London: Routledge.

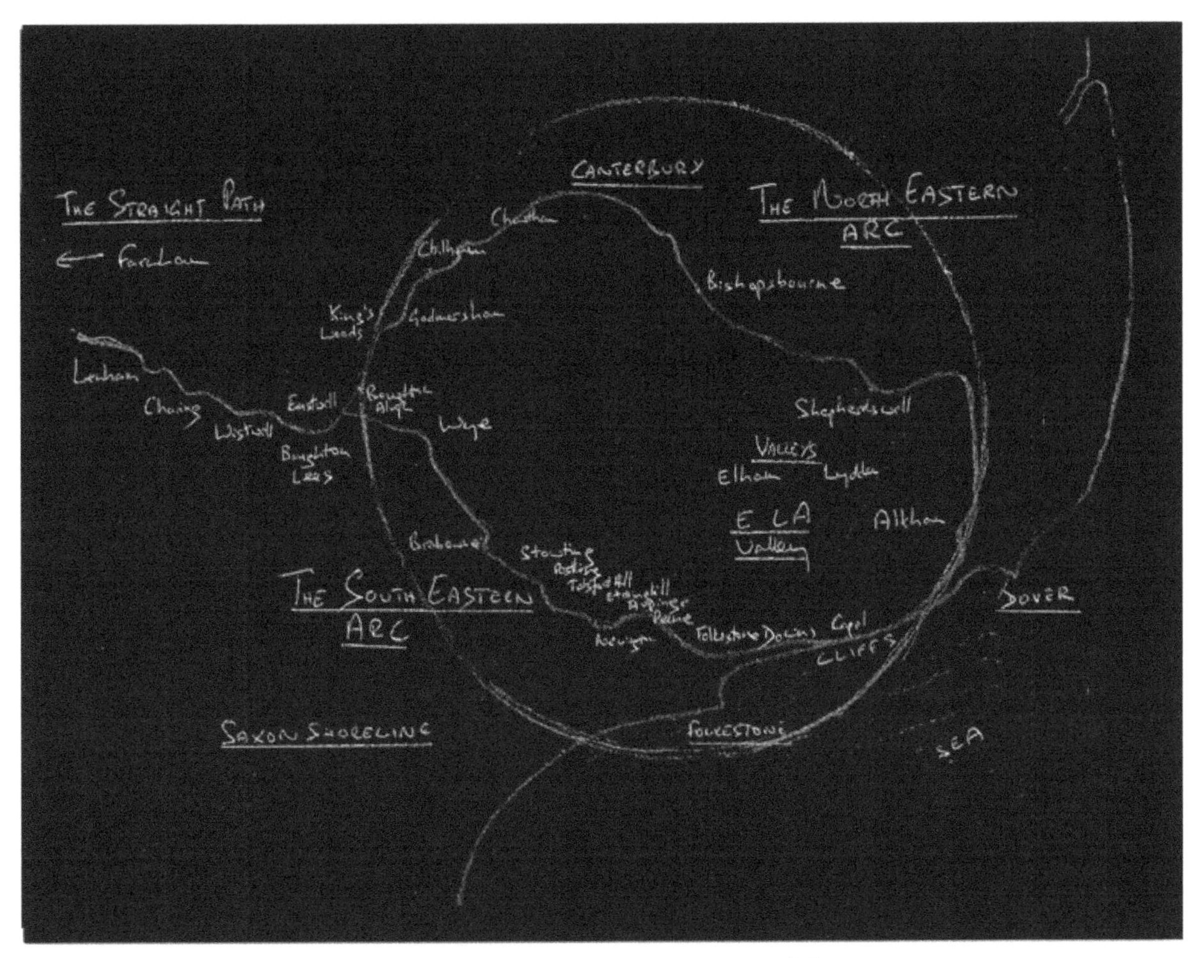

The North Downs' Eastern Ring as a Mandala

Walking

Why read anything at all into the act of walking,
except that it reads something into us,
makes us feel different, refreshed, smoothed out each time,
as if we had walked the body into liquid or transparency
and made our spirit strong.

And as if the spirit instructed by the body
was walking its journey into being,
not out of itself
but into.

~ 2 ~

THE STRAIGHT PATH

Lenham, Charing, Westwell, Eastwell

Journey's Beginning

The Pilgrims' Way starts in Winchester, meeting the North Downs Way at Farnham and continuing east until it splits near Boughton Aluph to go northeast through Canterbury to Dover, and southeast through the Folkestone Downs to Dover. Before the track leading from Farnham to Boughton Aluph reaches this circle, it has been relatively straight, with some slight meanders.

I jump onto it somewhere before but near this division as if I were boarding a train to my destination, which is my beginning at the point of its splitting.

There is much charm in the long straight-ish tracks characterising this part of the North Downs Way. In the lushness of summer foliage, they form dark tunnels as a welcome retreat from humidity, or in winter a refuge from sleet and rain. Often and characteristically, they run at a point someway down but parallel to the summit of the Downs, along the flanks, but are still sufficiently elevated to look out over flat lands spreading away from the base of the Down slopes. They are, of course, lovely but my purpose is to use their straight line to reach what I call Kent's North Downs' ring in the east.

The Pilgrim's Way, Charing to Westwell

Lenham

My random starting place on the 'straight' Way is near the War Memorial Cross on the Downs just above Lenham. It leads through Charing, Westwell and Eastway to reach the ring near Boughton Aluph. Although I am a walker, who gets there by car and joins a foot rather than rail track, I am its passenger all the same.

Lenham Lambs Unafraid

Profuse yellow of sun and prims and daffs. The White Cross looming above Lenham. The Pilgrim's Way, a tunnelled path. The end of it a stile we climb.

Physically, we follow a sign to Lenham Chalk Cliffs. Advice-wise, we follow a sign that says animals are frightened by dogs: *Be on the safe side and put your dog on the lead.* The lambs scatter from their mothers, then return and turn to look at us, unafraid. Although Dog isn't tugging to chase them, this is how the sheep should be. Unworried he's going to.

Across the tip of the sweeping, circling scarps and rounded coombes while lambs bleat and still stare, Dog helps me down the terraced slopes. At the bottom we open a gate. A sign reads: *Sheep worrying is an offence. Dogs found offending will be shot.*

A hunting bird screeches.

The sheep run to white plastic buckets filled with food.

On the loose chalk path, the first shimmer of spring heat rises. On my un-sleeved arms, I feel the first sun.

A lark sings his heart out, loudly. The open Downs take the fear away for a second like lambs un-chased by dogs. Relief and gratitude born. Dog's life on Down un-ended.

Holloway

Charing to Westwell

Entering a holloway east of Charing that passes along the top of Pett Lane on an already overcast humid day is to enter more darkness as well as being met with dark roots. There are gaps for looking out through the full foliage to ripe corn and barley fields stretching some distance away, but they are intermittant. When the sun does come out the contrast is upped between bright field and dark path, yet with the heightened bonus of dappled beams of dazzling sunlight to make the path look magical.

Each tree is distinctive, individual and while I walk on past them, they are still. The funnel is private, secret, personal, both protective and a little lurky and exposing. You'd be trapped if you met a robber.

In the distance, behind me, I hear voices. Their volume increasing rapidly suggests they aren't walking but whizzing on wheels. One is singing, 'And did those feet in ancient times' – music obviously to a Blake scholar's ears, but were they taking the piss out of a lone pilgrim and her dog? Suddenly four cyclists come from behind, throw friendly greetings and zoom past. Neither robbers nor piss-takers, they're just in genuine high spirits.

After exiting from the tunnel with the sun now fully out, both Dog and I feel too hot and so are relieved on the home run to enter the holloway again on the home run. In between, there was the sound of children playing, a bespoke campsite nearby, separated from us by a hedge. We are outside but not marginalised.

Finding again the dappled sunbursts that dazzlinge our path, I recall my children laughing and running around the garden when they were very young, magic years, so absorbing, you hardly know you're in them – and I make a point of saying this to the dappled sunbursts, so I will be with those times for ever.

Westwell to Eastwell

Westwell to Eastwell

Fir-tree arch in St Mary's church garden, Eastwell

On the last part of what I've called the 'straight' section of the North Downs before it reaches the circle, splitting at Boughton Aluph to go northeast, the way of the spirit, through Canterbury to Dover, and southeast, the way of the flesh, through Folkestone to Dover, trickles Westwell to Eastwell to Boughton Aluph.

Along this route lie the ruins of St Mary's church in Eastwell Park overlooking a lake. Its mortuary chapel is made of pure white chalk ashlar, its tower of flint and quoin, and its pointed archway is reflected by the green fir-arch in the picture of its garden. A tower just like one that has haunted my dreams, embedded in a forgotten lefthand corner of my home, a complex, fortress-like structure. It also reminds me of the house C.G. Jung built overlooking the lake at Bollingen called the 'Tower' (*Memories, Dreams and Reflections* 251) whose round fourfold structure came to represent psychic wholeness for him.

In another dream – before knowing my walk from Westwell would lead me to Eastwell's chapel and tower – I was swimming in a tidal pool with jaunty waves and rubber tyres and a woman who'd first become a mother at the same time as me. A great richness pervaded. One I'm reminded that hasn't ceased but needs replacing, as must one rubber tyre symbol-of-wholeness with another.

And, so, from Westwell to Eastwell I wend my way to find an arch opening onto water, a white chalk chapel, tower and lake, reminiscent of Jung's, behind me, and the joining of the two sides of the East Kent Downs, running from west to east on north and south sides, before me.

~ 3 ~

THE SOUTH EASTERN ARC

Wye, Brabourne, Stowting, Postling, Tolsford Hill and Scarps
Etchinghill Escarpment, Arpinge Escarpment, Peene
Folkestone Downs, Cherry Garden Hill and Cheriton Down, Castle Hill, Sugar Loaf Hill, Holywell, Wingate Hill, Dover Hill
The Warren , The Sea, Folkestone, Dover

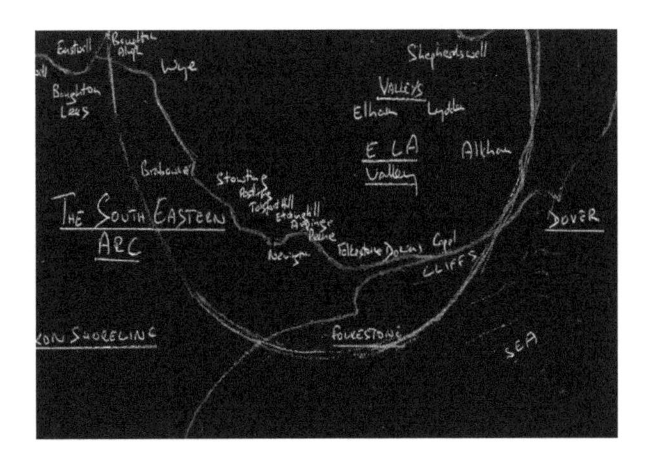

Wye

Why?

Jacob's Ladder

In his *Don Fernando*[*] book on Spain, Somerset Maugham discusses St Teresa, Spain's great mystic, asking, why should mysticism – something described as an awareness of a greater significance in the universe 'other than the known and above the unknown' – always be regarded as religious?

He has a point. After all, mysticism might be to do with our communion with nature as much as with God. Or the two might be regarded as inextricably linked. Certainly, I experienced some Wordsworthian moments of living *The Prelude* with my childhood friends high up on a hill – there were no mountains where we were – and found both. Okay, the North Downs isn't the landscape surrounding St Teresa in Avila, but any height can be numinous for a divine-in-nature-finding pantheist.

So, with child and teenagehood a prelude to other externals that follow, I still return to my beginnings, always if gladly left 'off' rather than out, going to higher ground in which the lower is most sacred and imbued, as the alchemists believed, with living spirit.

Right on cue there are steps from where I've parked the car at the end of Brook, just outside Wye, leading right to the top of the spur which forms one side of the Devil's Punchbowl on Broad Downs. Up we go, aided by the carefully laid timber, which meanders up the chalk incline to the summit. We are above the Punchbowl, looking into it and beyond.

A sign asks: '*Could this be the best view in Kent?*' One of them, could be the answer. We walk along the rim of the bowl dotted with May blossom and buttercups and descend another path which crosses over the road, through lush fields into Brook. When I look back, I see the chalk area cutting into the Downs on which our path had been laid and led us, like Jacob's ladder, to the top. ([*]Maugham, S., *Don Fernando,* Vintage, 2000, London (first published in 1935)

Devil's Punchbowl, Wye

Brabourne

Long Wood December

As with most walks there's no plan, or if there is, it's at the whim of other factors like weather, length of days, availability of sustenance, or who is coming. There's no expectation that words will be forthcoming. The prospect of a wood in winter while on our way across one end of a ridge to another, where the trees will be leafless, is fine but incidental.

We come across a white horse that stands looking at us from a milky peach and grey sunset in a picture taken some years ago, and now he turns to look at us again. He's so white, I say to black Dog, I could use him instead of you as a white, instead of black, pinprick on the landscape. Dog with his shiny black, brushed flanks is looking at the horse too, whose white is covered in blotches of mud and seems to say black and white look good together.

Go on, I say to Dog, turn right down your usual track into the woods. He cocks his head to make sure he's heard okay and offs it at a bound. Last time we were on this track, I remember coming out of it, not going in, the foliage thick with spring. He'd paused to peer through it with snout so definitely onto something serious that I'd paused to look through too and saw what had bombarded his senses: the birth smell of new calf popping out through its mother's slime onto the green ground. I felt exaltant as well as privileged to be there at that moment.

There may be no leaves but the sun is bright and cold and the slithering tree-trunks of snake or elephant grey are magnificent. Without the leaves I can hardly make out the path that's so familiar when in leaf or bluebell mode. Yet, the clear vista up to the edge of the woods and into fields brightly lit by the winter sun, is completely new. The former bluebell magic casts a different spell. The light is low but bright with an illumination summer can't achieve. The greens of sun on tiny patches of new bracken startle, while sunbursts, misty through fairy dust, chuck beams onto carpets of golden-brown leaves. Though there is no direct sun, the space between leafless branches is so large that the uplift of light over the distant slopes of the Pilgrim's and North Down Way's contours penetrates right through.

I recall Long Wood's floor in spring, carpeted with bluebell, then garlic. And August full on with bramble, fern, fresh green and curving tree-trunks, a palimpsest floor of death, decay, growth and rebirth.

We're at the top of the woods now with views through these denuded trees, but instead of coming to the copse's end, we come into what feels like a third section of it; elegant upward and curving trunks throwing sharp, long shadows in continuation and response to the sunbeams hitting the softly-leafed earth. I'm sucked into this extraordinary world as if I were powerless, while Dog careers after sticks, skidding and turning in churned up leaves and throwing their trembling fibres into minute particles of hanging and floating light. Shadow to sun. Earth to heaven. Dullness to magic. Wordlessness even to thought. The bright heart might just as well be cold, neither empty nor desiring, with nothing and no-one able to match this piercing winter light as you look back on Long Wood from the base perched upon a bathed-in-golden ridge.

Brabourne Downs

Brabourne Downs

Sometimes the shapes of the mandala I carry with me, which are my and others' stories, flow out in over-flow without being invited. The lead-up to the Long Woods of Brabourne reminds me of the elevated curve of Clench Common outside where my mother lived in Marlborough. I'd wanted to take her there, show her new pathways I'd discovered in other parts of the Wiltshire landscape she would have loved as a landscape painter and walker. By then she was too old and frail, and never made it, as she never made this place I cherish now.

But in these out-flows of memory she isn't absent and I consider how she whetted my appetite for walking long before she couldn't join me. Have I whet my childrens'? As kids they were taken to almost every county, to walk, to imbibe the freshness of air and then to pub. One abiding memory is of my daughter refusing to get out of the car at the base of Snowdon, and my boy throwing himself down a hillock at same base, when his broken ankle was only just out of plaster. They're great walkers now.

These snippets of memory colour a mandala where I'm alone but not lonely, like patches worked into a quilt alongside the wellbeing of Dog and I, up here in the rhythm and sun and long-viewed vistas, as intimations of how everything that ever was is ever now.

But where is the entrance to Long Woods shave? The North Downs Way path has swept by it, just at the place I saw the calf being born. Now, when I turn around to find it, I'm met with barbed wire fencing and *Private Keep Out* signs barring me from my most beloved of bluebell woods. They spoke of home when I'd been away and where I was first made breathless in Kent by sights of sapphire spreading cyanosis-coloured carpets spreading endlessly, little bigger than a shave. I'd already looked at other paler blue woods before returning to this one as if on a long overdue visit to a precious, intensely blue-eyed friend going the other way. From the darkness of friendship to its light.

Well, if I've lost Long Woods, the fact strikes home I have lost the companionship of my mother and in some ways, my children. My first instinct is to ring up the farmer and explain I need to photograph my bluebell woods in the spring, leaving out the word 'my', but realise this might be as ludicrous as asking him to reseed my mother.

A chap on the track with two dogs puts this in perspective when I ask him if he knows who owns the woods. He said he had tried to find out but is resigned to the fact the farmer doesn't want anyone in there, not just bikes, but us too, he supposes and 'that's that'.

I don't always think 'that is that' but let it go as I must also, apparently, with places, people and creatures of intimate preciousness, and take heart that the North Downs Way metaphor for everything that can't be taken away with *Private* signs as far as I know. How beautiful is this elevation overlooking flat land out to the South Downs through smoke-filled skies from winter fires and over the boldly undulating spurs – gigantically fluted and fissured – of Brabourne Downs. Dog has just been streaking over them, a black dog-dot racing, tracing their sumptuous sunlit curves.

Both woods and words can be privatised, if necessary, but those of us who don't own woods can own our own words instead and choose to keep them open, free and public.

But whoops, while the man is talking to me, unbeknown to us, Dog has mounted his black and white collie.

'Don't do that!' he exclaims.

I'd not known she was a bitch on heat, and we both agree we hoped he'd not done 'that'.

'Although... why not?' I couldn't resist saying. 'They'd make beautiful puppies.'

Then I explained (though he was hardly listening by now as he knew I was alluding to a not necessarily desired future) that Dog, being a cross between collie and German shepherd, would make the perfect father of gorgeous offspring. Instead, he said he'd keep *schtum* about it when it came to 'the wife' as if he was warming to the idea. I couldn't think of a time Dog had had such an easy advantage with owners distractedly talking to each other.

Although they've taken away 'my' bluebell woods, I'll remember there are many others and, because the North Downs Way is protected, no part of it can suddenly be declared private. It's a clear run like other ways and walking routes around the country, and I see it as a golden thread reflecting my children's' lives, meandering safely for them, and all countryside lovers through today's soft and yielding air.

Stowting

The Tiger

People might know Stowting by its Tiger Inn, one of the few buildings on the main street running through the village. I know this too, but I'm beginning to discover the meadows and streams around the Tiger, wondering what 'immortal hand or eye can frame their fearful symmetries', no doubting that in the pretty lanes and fields of Stowting, seasons and reasons are treacherous whims.

So, the too deep mud which has made many paths impassable in winter is replaced by the too deep grass which also impedes progress. We follow path-like routes of flattened stems, only to have to turn back, or forge our own flattening. Nevertheless, they are lovely and Dog, the cross-pollinator, must leap over them like a kangaroo, loosening pollens to fly up into the air with him.

The stream I'd been thinking to bring Dog to bound and splash his heat away in is mostly blocked off by thorns and stinging nettles. Coming through one gate, I'm snared by brambles, but rather than rip myself free, I extricate myself slowly, revolving around and away from painful suckers and worse scratchings. The lesson, not to confront the bramble that grabs.

Trying to follow a path over the stream's small bridge, Dog turns back before me. He is right. He knows neither of us can easily get through the brambles, thorns and nettles growing higher than me and we cannot see far enough along it to guess at its ending. I'd set out today with the feeling we'd have a short walk over some glorious summer pastures, but my legs are stinging from the nettles and thorns.

That's one side to the ground. The other is thick, lush, or sheep and cow short-grazed with large daisies, shastar or gerber leaping from the long grasses. I'd anticipated this wouldn't be a long walk and wouldn't change me much. But it has. I can feel the energy left by movement course through my body, so good above my doubting in Stowting. Coming into sumptuous summer seasons and reasons all about for changing us too.

Postling

Going east from Wye, with its spectacular V-shaped Devil's Kneading Trough coombe, whose banks and spurs have been grazed for centuries, and whose grasslands are said to be amongst the most flower rich in the country, the North Downs Way ridge meanders through Brabourne and Stowting to Postling. This ridge with its steep banks of scarp provide some of the most impressive viewpoints in Kent – overlooking lands of the Pent, the Stour Valley, the Channel and the French coast – with Tolsford Hill close by.

Joseph Conrad lived at the base of Pent Down at Pent Farm. Perhaps the artist Walter Crane and poet Christina Rossetti walked where we walk, celebrating the landscape as we do.

Sun Games

Kiss chase is the game Dog and I play with the December sun as it scatters its rays over Pent Downs at daylight's last and finest hour. It has streaked over the fields and across my head so low, even at three in the afternoon, and so blindingly bright that it pierces my eyes and makes it hard to see while driving, strobing through the trees at an agitating rate like speed cameras flashing on and off, over and over again. This kiss chase is two-way, us chasing the sun and it catching us between wanting to hold it here and let it go.

Boots touch an unreliable ground as Dog and I stride out over squelching patches of mud pooled by gates through bitterly cold winds, the orb beckoning regardless, sharp against the furrow's shadows, shattering out of an intense blue surround. Dog romps in its glory as if we've got all day, and we don't hurry, the sun impressively getting brighter as it lowers, shots of little cloud like warning signs appearing suddenly on a clear horizon, muffling the sun with shadow momentarily, then letting it go to tease us before its final disappearance behind the hill.

We might have walked to the next hill and then another were it not for the absent torch. Our chasing sunlight game on this stage, whose audience is an undulating landscape, has helped us use time to see how far we can go before the curtain finally comes down. But now it needs to be brought to a close. Almost tripping into the deepening shadows of a muddy path contouring the hill in terracettes, helps me decide. Very soon must we flee the big bad devouring darkness flying on the heels of the dying sun, yet still we are bewitched by the light on the scarp and in the downland grasses as it passes through spectrums of red, gold and apricot. Peach down flanked behind it, Dog runs before a silhouetted tree. Then the shade takes control altogether of this part of our earth, along with the immutable, smooth, stillness of the hills, slightly menacing but not yet opaque. Breath-taking, once for Conrad too.

Postling church spire rises from behind the hill - and Dog and I cross it to the car before darkness engulfs us. It's four o'clock. We've had this best one hour of chase and kiss light, and now the sun, not I, is the ginger-bread man saying you can't catch me, my ginger's gobbled up and I've gone *down under*, while inside the car we snake-sneak our way back along roads to different, e-lec-tric, light, *up over*.

Pent Downs

Lower Postling

I have plumped for a flat, hopefully uninterruptable stretch under Postling after a rather frustrating stop-start walking in Stoke Newington and Streatham the day before yesterday. Turning right off a straight track onto and across a gently swelling grassy, sheep-filled field we come to several stiles. Dog has been very docile, walking for some time through sheep scattering before or following us, running round to our left in groups as if ganging up against us, before scattering off again.

But, at the stiles, he's impatient and I'm annoyed with him like yesterday in London when he tugged me to every smell, yanking my arms out of their sockets. So, this time, instead of allowing him to barge past me while I'm trying to climb the stile, I get him to sit and wait. Behind a stile and a little bridge over a brook and another stile he waits, very good, before my 'come' which propels him up and over like a graceful pony at a gymkhana.

Seeing his beauty and moved again by his sensitive intelligence, all is forgiven. To help me get over my crossness, he puts on an entertainment, tugging at bits of cut, spikey crop in a field to see if he can pull them out to use as a stick for me to throw, and while I'm looking for another that's not so flimsy we've actually found a way down to the East Stour River. Usually covered in undergrowth now chopped down by a tractor, Dog runs in and out to keep me amused. Along the track back there are paths I want to check out, I tell him. He stops at each one as if asking, 'shall we go up this?' and when I say, no thanks, off he trots again until he's (impatiently) a long way ahead of me. But before I've said anything, he's stopped, checked where I am, and come running back, so I tell him he's good and helpful today, and still he keeps on stopping to look back at my progress till I find a good-sized stick. I'm amazed to be having this conversation with him, that he checks out the paths I'd been talking about, that he waits for me and understands my words. I am in awe of what a creature he is in all this.

Off the open track now a clump of trees, bigger than a tott, attracts me to its twisted trunks and deep, dark recessions under its branches stretching over the ground. My mind is empty. The mind is lonely. The mind is strong. Strength is lonely. But, hey, this is where I find my mind, myself, prompted by the shapes of trees, curving paths, inclines. This is me, privileged to have it before me. But where is everyone? Why aren't people cavorting through the sinuous undulations of this foliage? Stroking the soft leaves? Rolling in the luscious grass of this open countryside?

And for a second there's an over-egged feeling that all this is a terrible mistake. That every part of nature speaks to us of some goodness within and without the psyche we have neglected, abandoned, and now stands derelict apart from each of us singularly walking through it, glimpsing for an even shorter second a long-lost beauty which was once part of us.

I thought of this place this morning and here it is, giving me an empty mind that is full, a craziness full with gratitude. My consciousness, my light, devoid of people, replaced by the topography seen from the base, not tops of hills, where my eyes might feast on the familiar outlines. Tolsford Hill, Postling Down.The woods at the top of 'Conrad's quarry'. All this can't be just for me, unless it's in my mind, which it isn't.

This holds true even if Dog and I are pummel-tired from our pavement pounding in the city, perhaps even because of it. And what also holds true is the two-way passage between us and this place. Have I projected these moments onto the landscape or does it bestow them upon me?

The next day, I park at the same spot and take some pictures of what was too dark yesterday. I walk away from the woods that had provided some epiphany in relative darkness, to the heights of Postling Down, though these moments, it becomes evident, still remain in yesterday's low, private, woody base.

Postling and the Lost Camera, July 2016

Day after day I came back to the same spot. The place is a soft, springy track made of weighed down hay, splaying out under my feet like a weave going in one direction in some places, then whirling off in another. This was where I took my last picture after which the camera was no more.

The track sloped down to the edge of a mowed-grass airstrip, then a hedge of brambles and nettles beside the East Stour River which I could not see. Then, a bridge which I wouldn't cross, another sheep or walker's path alongside the hedge to a heavy iron gate at the bottom of the field swollen with more brambles, nettles and thorns that I had to push my way through to open.

On the fateful day I'd flung down my stuff on the flattened foliage in order to heave up the heavy metal fastening of the iron gate, then thrown it down on the other side to close it. Leaning forcibly through more hostile overgrowns, Dog and I had found a little slanted, slatted bridge leading to the track we'd lost some half hour before that.

We've made it, I'd said to Dog, but when a few yards further down the track I threw my stuff down again to take stock, my camera wasn't there. Though I was exhausted, we turned back, it must be by the gate, I'd thought. But it wasn't. So, it had to be after the hay track, I concluded, only just remembering the very last shot I'd taken. But it wasn't.

Since then, we've scoured those few yards every day.

My latest loss must mean something. Either that I'm not to be trusted with a possession I've just spent ninety pounds to replace a scratched lens and therefore shouldn't take pictures anymore, or that I should buy a better camera and be more responsible. The fact I want it to mean something is obviously to help alleviate the upset, not so much for the item itself, but for the pictures recording memories I cherish. I can only commit their memory now to word on paper as a way of remembering, though I will never know what crackers in contrasting drama and ambience there might have been.

The pictures were a record I made of a journey I made when I left the sea, knowing, hoping, I would be back. That no accident would befall us to stop our return. To the sea. We may be moored to the landward side of the littoral, poised between liquid and solid, but what, to recollect Conrad, do chance, passion, commerce, endeavour or action stand, when all about us is always the magnetic sea? The shine of the sun slicing into its splash and suck through a sharp blue summer's sky.

The journey had been made when I wasn't in love with love but topography, the shapes and patterns on the surface of our land, changing and undulating as much as we do. So what were the photographs I took?

An undiscovered avenue of beech trees off the motorway near what had once been my mother and father's home I'd known very well in Wiltshire, Dog running down it.

A gushing brook under a tunnel of trees in Stroud, Dog running through it.

A tent the colour of back-ground earth before the Long Wynd and Stiplestones in Shropshire, Dog running across it.

Backlit fronds of barley and fields of golden corn, Dog running across them.

Silhouettes against dramatic horizontals, anti-silhouettes against the same. A life-size Buddha beside a hedge, Dog barking at it, once, then sniffing the Buddha's face.

My sister's dogs with Dog.

The place I come back to on the path of trampled hay is near Pent Farm where Joseph Conrad lived. Apart from jamming my fingers in the bathroom door at my sister's house, I had arrived safely from this trip back at the sea without incident. When I lost my camera, I pricked that same finger with a thorn. To begin with, I realise this was Conrad's countryside. Nor had I given consideration to the possibility that Walter Crane was here, along with a Rossetti.

When I started my journey away from the sea, I'd heard on the radio that a priest's throat had been slit inside a church. That my four-year old great nephew had got leukaemia. The priest had been a humble assistant administering the sacrament to two nuns.The child, a long time in coming gift to tired but over-joyed parents. This information made horror-hills in my valley of peace, putting downs into my beautiful topography of ups. I might have said that against this the loss of my camera pales, but, instead, I acknowledged the grief, the loss of moments, making an offering each day through my visit to a site where a thing went missing. Not to placate but to bring into full view grieving moments lost to sight, pictures not seen, catastrophes striking.

This spot I come back to day after day is by the conjunction of my path beside the East Stour River with a track that stretches west to east along the valley. Its brambles have scratched my legs and made them bleed, but not stopped planes take off from its airstrip.

I have wanted to have a 'spot', a place to return to, now it has claimed me. But if I had done the claiming, it would have been at the up of the Downs, instead of the down of down here. I had wanted to have a place to return to, unsuspecting it would be a scene of loss like a shrine.

Today, I go to the heights above it, the place I might have chosen, the meandering and flowing combines of coombe and spur, the curve and wind from which I can see it all from sea through clumps of tree landmarks and scarps furrowed by shadow, through dips and ridges, dene, spinney, to the toll of Brockman's Bushes at Etchinghill. From this elevated perch, I look down on the shadow of clouds rolling over the valley where my camera might be buried or smashed, so I am wary still of extolling this panorama for the moment and wonder if something else is gone too – until pulled back from the elsewhere by an urgent whinny of horse filling the air, which gets answered by neigh from another field.

Cows round a bend on a track through totts of lovely long grasses, but they aren't mooing, rather threatening as they come stampeding towards us like elephants trumpeting out of a jungle. And running away from this Dog and I return to the flat lows in search of my image-maker camera now imaginary.

We do the usual track back, the heavy metal gate, the whirling splays of hay. But what Dog finds today at the end of the hostile track brambled and nettled with thorny branches reaching horizontally across it, tarmacked here and there (once an important thoroughfare) are several paths through scratchy undergrowth to what feels like a secret brook, actually a river, babbling like fury, that we can hear and see glistening through the spiky foliage. Dog slithers by the weapons without being wounded, cools his pads with a relieving temperature servicing his whole body under dark, sun-attracting fur, drinks to quench his thirst and chases a stick with exaggerated splashing flourishes.

As we pass through the gate, we're aware of a couple of small planes circling over us, as if we're being watched, wondering if we need to keep clear at the end of the runway should they want to land. But squinting at them in the bright sky, head tilted back, they disappear into the clouds until the rumble of their engines getting quieter vanishes altogether. I wonder if there's another landing strip nearby. But, by now, we're making our way, camera-less, back to the car, and here comes the wonderful sound of pounding hooves galloping on hollow earth. Horses alarmed by our sudden footsteps in the field beside our path.

Postling, the Lost Camera, Conrad and The Heart of Darkness

One day, reminding myself that Conrad worked on *The Heart of Darkness* in the farm nestling at the base of Postling Downs, just across these fields with tracks that criss-cross over the Stour Valley, I put my camera-search tracks on hold., convincing myself that I share something with Conrad. We both obfuscate the usual pattern of logic. He with his *The Heart of Darkness* which is a blow to the constraints of what appears to be an ordered, rational, western world, and I with the disappearance of an object I knew to be there, lying down in a valley where I search in vain. What is it I hope to find, Conrad himself? Besides and by *The Heart of Darkness* we are shocked time and again by evil, illness, mortality. With this thought instilled but put to one side, I walk up towards Postling Woods where the land stretches out to sea and bay in patchwork, copse and ripe-to-bursting fields of crop or smooth furrowed lines of tractor on harvested ones.

What passages there are in *The Heart of Darkness* that I have started reading for yet another time. Page six. *The water shone pacifically; the sky, without a speck, was a benign immensity of unstained light ... What greatness had not floated on the ebb of that river [Thames] into the mystery of an unknown earth!.. the dreams of men, the seed of commonwealth, the germs of empires.* This, Marlow comments, had been one of the *dark places of the earth.* If light, like Knights or Drake, came from this river after the Romans, it was only like a blaze on the plain or a flash of lightning in the clouds – *We live in the flicker* – darkness was here yesterday. Conquerors dependent on the weakness of others use brute force and robbery with violence. The conquest of the earth means taking it away from those who look different. *Not a pretty thing when you look into it too much.*

Every time I read *Heart of Darkness* I find something different. Despite the *implacable force* always being there *brooding over an inscrutable intention,* new meanings each time, ones that were there before, gone. *It is impossible to convey the life-sensation of any epoch of one's existence – that which makes its truth, its meaning – its subtle and penetrating essence. It is impossible. We live, as we dream – alone.* As a teenager in the wake of travels to Africa I understood *The Heart of Darkness* to be about the evils of repressed 'instinct', whereas now I can see it about the compassion of Marlowe's white lie in telling Kurtz' 'intended' that the last words he uttered were her name, not *the horror, the horror* as was really the truth of it.

My perspective has shifted. My lion now is lying down with my lamb. A read book like a taken path different each time it is attempted. And I have trod the track over Brabourne further west more times than I have read Conrad. Off it I may be denied Long Wood's spring carpet of bluebells, then garlic, its summer's fresh green fern fronds striking postures against curling tree-trunks and screen vicious brambles, its palimpsest floor of death and growth, but like the re-read book the re-trodden track winds on through other meanings and woods just like thee, from ego perhaps to empathy, in the case of the white lie.

In *Heart of Darkness* Marlow/Conrad's perspective has changed too. The blank spaces of the earth on the map he'd put his finger on as a child lost to the glories and glamour of exploration became places of darkness as an adult. An immense river like an uncoiled serpent with its head in the sea, its body curving over the land towards a tail lost in its depths, had charmed him like a snake a bird. Small correspondence, but here I have the East Stour River, and don't seek to enslave.

I hover over highly visible imagery: *I saw a face amongst the leaves on the level with my own, looking at me very fierce and steady and then suddenly, as if a veil had been removed from my eyes, I made out, deep in the tangled gloom, naked breasts, arms, legs, glaring eyes – – the bush was swarming with human limbs in movement, glistening, of bronze colour. The twigs shook, swayed and rustled.* I am pre-occupied not with a prime minister's reference to immigrants as 'swarming' but with averting my eyes from the tangle of foliage cutting me off from this tributary of the East Stour.

What reason can there be that conquest is horror and slavery rather than discovery, that the child is ill, the priest is killed, and I have done no worse than lose my camera? If I've lost the ability to record have I also to 'seeing'. The reality is that the child will go through gruelling treatments, chemo, lumber punctures, steroids and be unable to walk. The priest has lost consciousness to the world for ever. I will probably never see my camera again nor those photographs of a life lived lovingly framed. But always it's the overriding picture of us as plunderers, unable to turn back from the distress we've caused, that's missing.

The case of 'lost things found by chance' hasn't happened with my camera, but by chance, Conrad's *Chance* is set very close to where I am now, at a chalk pit, Hempton Hill Quarry. I will try to reach it through more brambles and briars. Because, says Marlow in *Chance,* the science of life consists in seizing every possible chance that presents itself! Yet on a bad day, thoughts, like some pathways, lead nowhere, and though from a field to the west of Postling Down, I tried to reach the wooded chalk quarry I'd had found no way through the tight, barbed wire fencing. Some days later I resolved to enter the quarry from the *road winding up the hill out of which it had been excavated.*

The quarry is the site Marlow mentioned in *Chance* where Flora is tempted to suicide. *One day he saw a woman walking about on the edge of a high quarry, which rose a sheer hundred feet, at least, from the road winding up the hill out of which it had been excavated.* He'd shouted out a warning of the danger, and she'd retreated among some young Scotch firs near the brink of the precipice.

The speed of traffic along this road was unprecedented, but bracing myself against the terror of it took my 'chance' and entered this dappled, half-enchanted, half-spooky scrub with the Scotch firs Conrad mentioned towering high above its edge with huge chalky drops. They weren't as sheer as they might have been but were dirtied by many a human mark, go-cart, bicycle or other track scratched into a surface and eroded by footprint and weather since Conrad's time. I too ran down the white chalk, my thoughts, like the pathway into this wood, opened by the possibility that Conrad had been here, the many meetings, sinister or otherwise, that had taken place here, then try as I may, even with Dog's help, I couldn't get up the steep bank. Half-way up to the top, the surface too loose and steep to get a grip, I slid down it. Small new fir trees on the brink drenched in sunshine still beckoned, along with the field peeking through between them.

We found a footpath across another field through horses, Shetland ponies and sheep to the edge of the forest at the top, but still the sunshine summit which had beckoned us, was out of bounds beyond more tight, barbed wire fencing and vicious brambles. But we are near enough and I think again about the young woman spotted by Marlow in *Chance* at the top of the high chalk pit. Why was she trying to kill herself? It wasn't love, rather her father's ruined fortunes and her callous carers at a time when women had little resources of their own. And an echo of *Heart of Darkness'* existential 'horror'?

A year later, at the end of August, I return to the scene where text has no supportive photographs. The track is even more grown over than last year and the horses unimpressed by our return. The huge gate with the heavy metal lock is still there, but so tightly packed with brambles, it's not worth the effort of opening, so we follow the other route along the East Stour River, invisible because of the thickness of foliage.

What a revelation. The whole spectacle of Pent Down, from the top of the chalk quarry along the upper flanks of the Down and round to Tolsford Hill spreads before us, the runway its gateway, no interruptions to its summit. And now this whole open stretch with significant Down landmarks in my Ring, so familiar to my plodding feet and downturned gaze, is interesting because I'm writing about it rather than documenting it visually as with the other landmarks.

Lost in my search for the lost, I wonder if my writing has been myopic, fixated, walk after walk, in following the exact footsteps we'd trodden, sure that the camera would appear as if by some miracle of my own deciding. Instead this fertile countryside proves something about projection and perception as an awareness I didn't have this time last year opens up before me in the landscape. Every bump on the surface of the Down's horizon behind Conrad's Pent Farm is heightened and flowing one into the other, the chalk quarry, the chalk scarp, the chalk summit of the Pent Down, the lovely swell of softly blowing grass on the slope leading down from Etchinghill's mast, and the tree-covered steepness of Tolsford Hill.

So what? I say to myself. Why should this matter? Am I going crazy? Can I really consider these old friends? And what of people? Where are they? Everywhere. Am I looking for solace in hills because people have disappointed me or let me down? They haven't!

Now the scene of my crime which has been rectified because of the insight is to be recorded with another camera and a picture of the ground; an implacable force brooding over an inscrutable intention behind Conrad's farm; a gate which looked too hard to open that led to a new path, and a tiny glimpse of the East Stour River. A track in water that flows with leaves upon it like leaves within a book or a path taken on leaf litter. A meaning I've found in Conrad of a new crime that is old.

Tolsford Hill and Scarps

Showerless at Tolsford

If a scud is a quickly passing shower, the one I can see as we begin an ascent towards Tolsford Hill from the Postling side, had better stay in the distance I say to Dog, trying to gauge whether the direction of the wind is for or against us. But if it is a virga – a visible shaft of rain that evaporates before reaching the ground – as a clearly delineated grey chunk of cloud in the distance descending with feathery bits hanging down from it, looks to be, it shouldn't strike us.

But there is too much going on in the sky, and winds seeming to come from one angle, then another, make it difficult to be sure of anything. It's not dintless – that is cloudless, but nor is there any sense of dropples, that is – large drops of rain. It looks like it could be gleamy, meaning showers with fitful sunshine, but all we have, at the moment, is a bright sharpness that lures us upwards through lush green September grass.

We turn left to go up the western slope that skirts Tolsford's wood, scrambling under hawthorn and chalky inclines till we find a path sunk into the terracettes that look inland on this side of the hill. But instead of following this contour, Dog decides to go through the stile onto the side of the hill overlooking St Mary's Bay to Dungeness, following round the other edge of the clump of trees that we could call a toll or a pett. The grey sky hanging 'thing' which I've decided to call a virga is still there but is floating seawards rather than towards us.

We scramble along some deeply etched tyre-marks through more lush grass and sheep, steering clear of a blood-curdling shriek that after a few listens I decipher to be a man's not cows' or sheep, and chancing upon a nonchalant family of three out black-berrying with a ladder, decide it must have been one of them, the teenage boy, troubled perhaps, rather than a murder victim.

The virga, as we start heading back towards the toll or pett, still hangs in the sky, closer towards the sea now, its feathery trails as light as ever. It hasn't eclipsed the sun which shines bright and sharp with an autumn intensity over the Tolsford Hill side overlooking buttressing scarps to the full trees that gather above Postling. The scarps' shadows are deep. Hawthorn bushes bright in the sun.

We have travelled this little way through sharp and brightly-almost-blinding weather that hasn't hurt us, and rounded the same bend back to the car, feeling a little transformed in our lungs by fantastical sky worlds with the virga still kindly at bay. We have had a proper soodle or a prole – which is a (very) pleasurable short walk.

Weather

Winter storms with gale force winds have been raging for weeks
rather than days.
And while the heaving and crashing open sea is one
the one firmament above it is made up of many scuds
floating piecemeal in a broadly patterned sky.
The forces of water fall they carry varies.
Heavy, squally or vaporous, in drifting mists of sea.
Gagey. Gleamy.
No form will last long, as much as the blue sky won't.
That everything will quickly transform into something else
the only blustering certainty.

Still a scud is not a sckud when it has changed
from a lightly, quickly passing shower to a deluge
and the horizon and patchwork sky once bursting in shafts of light
can no longer be seen.
Nor is a frisk or shatter a scattering or a sprinkling of rain when it
has become a heavy, continuous flist.

Golden winter afternoon

The circle whether mandala, ring or soul that is all-encompassing embraces memory and space without having all of either. So the sunken track or holloway that goes up Tolsford Hill reminds me of the ancient Fosse Way that ascends the Mendip Hills where once we lived, but that is all.

I don't need to spend time visiting this subjective site because being here on Tolsford Hill is more enticing. Because the circle that revolves and reminds rewinds, winds up and winds on, we not falling off the wheel nor yet going around in circles. Concentricity is various not duplicitous or repetitive. To touch all its layers would be like claiming we knew every blade of grass or pebble on the beach.

At the top of this Fosse-like track we are on the flanks of the chalk Downs. We follow their sinuous curves, the grass again golden in the late afternoon winter light. The gently rolling spiral we seem to walk on frames the rest of the country on one side, the sea to the other. And then we are tumbling down the softly-tussocked hill to a pretty little path that leads through some woods and on to a muddy field peppered already by fresh sprigs of green crop, and round back to the path we first thought of, in a loop.

I didn't learn about the Tolsford Barrows until I got home. The Fosse Way of my once-life is Roman and has led back to these burial mounds of Late Neolithic to Late Bronze Age (2400-1500 BC) which I missed today but will look for another time, just feeling now how rich this concentricity is, with me, popped here in a momentary middle.

Summerhouse Hill

A tongue licking out from the Down-ridge by a fault line that once shifted its chalk.
An old-fashioned sugar loaf made of gault and limestone.
A cone formed by erosion of rain and wind separated from other ridges.
Geology and history meeting in perception, poetry and meditation.
By crack, slip or erosion did Britain once separate from Europe.

Summerhouse Hill

Etchinghill Escarpment

Existential Etchinghill

Okay, I say to Dog, time to go out. But, as he who is always at the mercy of humans' indecisions suspects, there's one more thing to do, write down, think about, gather up, before going out becomes reality. Sometimes I feel sorry for him. All he can do is trust, and trust again, if necessary that his trust will be reborn: that my procrastination will come to an end. That I won't turn into an ogre. All too easy against a 'dumb', trusting creature.

Only a temporary glitch of a thought. All I've said is it's time to go out, but not gone yet. Look at Dog and I. What matters to him matters to me, simple things counting to simple natures lucky to be hell-bent on this outing which changes them.

But it's hard work walking, or hard working over the walking mud. It slides under feet and paws like a conveyor belt that's gone askew. All is December grey. Yet the fallow woodland floor once bursting with bluebell and garlic still excites Dog, and me too. The cracking twigs, Dog's rasping, excited breaths. Throw me the stick again, he's saying, again and again and again. For through The Beeches, as these woods are called, spidery tracks forged through brown twigs and green leaves, hidden in summer by dense foliage, now stretch their tentative fingers out across the floor. Now there are spaces to throw a stick, a winter glade strewn only with a fallen horizontal trunk of curling, once vertical tree. Dog skids through the brown beech and oak leaves, flinging them and their dust up into the air as he stops to twist and return, disturbing the damp, peat earth underneath, but retrieving the stick.

Whispering woods. Whispering words. The susurrating wind whoops them up, rushing from an unseen distance in an unknown ether. Voluminous spinneys of beech trees with mazes of high branches play host to itinerant winds. Dog keeps snapping the brittle but flimsy branchlets and dry leaves under paw as he chases one whim after another over a million seasons laying down their ever-compressing layers of underlay beneath this carpet.

The glitch returns. Humans starting out happy, enthusiastic, giving their all, then by slow degrees allowing themselves to feel quashed, let down, one thing then another neither valued nor wanted, taken out, trodden underfoot. The human heart brought down, disappointed, growing cold. Yet the sounds and presences of wind and snapping twigs in this woodland are not of people, and this decomposing forest floor is recomposing into something new that's alive and bursting on a grim winter's day.

Within this long but narrow toll, a pett, perched on the edge of a scarp, a brent on the brow of the hill, is fallow land resting before spring. A humble nab on one side of a horseshoe spur drops steeply down one way, flowing gently down another, from which we glimpse sides of the Downs and sloping fields, also sleeping, that we won't be following today.

For the uneven, rain-sodden paths have been turned to stew, totts of otherwise solid grass reduced to high mounds that sink like putty under wellington boots squashling through slappy dough. A zam-zody if we were in Exmoor, our spandled foot and paw prints too widely dissolved and loose to be recognisable. I'm tired of it, I say to Dog again, trudging and repetitive in thought and body, with the exhaustion of perpetually trying not to slip and find myself face down in mud. So, he comes up beside me to lend support, and I cling to his collar for steadiness. Then we've rounded the bend, avoiding sheep to our left, and Dog takes off chasing rabbits in and out of the prickly gorse bushes, leaving me clinging now to the fence, my stumbling, fumbling feet seeking out the steadier grassier edges of the quagmire, tottering towards the totts.

I feel weak, I say to Dog. Ooh, how he yawns, and we look again at the shapes of coombes and spurs in the grey winter light that have inspired us in the summer, the steep inclines that we won't do today but will instead keep focussed on the level to avoid the ascents and descents for those not feeling strong.

We cross a field with a little domesticated hawmell (the old Kent word for a paddock) separated from those inspiring curving slopes of wind-rustled long grasses that we've luxuriated through on balmy sunshine days and can still glimpse through the open trees. A flisk, a shatter of light rain, touches us, the wind still suthering through the distant trees more loudly than the fizmer, which is also visible as well as audible, shifting in ripples through the gossamer grasses, much as it does at times every season in this place we love. The drizzle fizzles, the scud passes.

On the way back through those whispering, windy, wonderful woods, I release a neat little stick into the large spaces between trunks. It spins wildly out of control, bouncing off a tree and landing at its feet. Down on it as if he were killing a rat, Dog imprisons the thing, clamping it into his quivering, jaunty jaw, tossing it into the air, turning it around nonchalantly in his mouth so it twirls as if he were a cheerleader with a baton.

He never stops to ask if the abandoned leaf really can be cheered to know it's part of the forest's regeneration. If the disappointed human heart grows colder than fallow, Dog's doesn't. In as much as I take a long time about it Dog trusts I'll carry on doing what I do, and I'll do my utmost not to let him down.

Etchinghill Summit

Spell-binding fluffs of cloud swell to crown a 360-degree view. To the east beyond Sugar Loaf, Round and Castle Hill the Martello Tower on Folkestone's East cliff. Straight out south in front The Grand and The Metropole. To the northeast, the Arpinge escarpment; and right out to sea going west, St Mary's Bay, windmills, Fairlight and the South Downs. Turning northwest, the bigger body of the North Downs stomping towards Farnham, and other outlines I'm not sure of, right the way back round to eddies of hills flowing out behind Arpinge.

Etchinghill Escape

If you need to escape the clutter of the day, go up to Etchinghill escarpment, parking under Swingfield Radio Mast. We did, but today find our plateau peaked with cows scattered widely rather than in a group, making more space unavailable than there would have been had they been in a small tight clump like Brockman's Bushes from which they circled outwards right across the biggest field. Over-reacting a little perhaps but there'd been stories recently and I didn't want Dog and I 'dead by cow'.

Forced to mandala around them, dosey doe, we're jettisoned into other fields and woods that unravel new vistas and pathways. First to the side that overlookings the valley of Etchinghill up to the Arpinge escarpment, then south as usual over the Leas across La Manche to France. Then round the familiar Brockman's Bushes, peering into them, and to their other side with Summerhouse Hill caught in a haze, behind where Dog has a naughty skirmish with a bullock, black like him.

And, so, to escape, it we drop off the summit as we proceed west to find some springy paths through totts leading under and through hawthorns, many a teasing rabbit scampering away from Dog, then up again before bearing north behind the line of trees separating us from the cows leading onwards on the North Downs Way towards Pent Down.

Shadow-sumed flanks of Down stand firm as rock though I think of shifty-shaky sand dunes. Paths forged by animal and human cut through bounteous fields of deep ripe grass, the sort of paths you can walk down without seeming to progress – till we're quite loathe to turn home but must now we're girded round with the cardinal points and this particular Etchinghill mandala is complete.

Arpinge Escarpment

From Holy Well to Arpinge Heights

The field from Holywell Avenue to Holywell is muddy, but not as muddy as the path. The noise of traffic from the base of Sugar Loaf Hill is distracting and as dirty as the mud. Not alarmingly loud, but just taking away all possibility of calm, as if every peaceful air molecule in this protected horseshoe combe were instead amplifying sound.

Only, in flits of occasional sunshine, the almost thick foliage veiling Holywell's water is a relief counterbalance to the stagnate stench and feel of mud as it glues itself to my boots and Dog's underbelly.

But Holywell can always hold its own, even though the traffic still gives no relief, nor the mud. Known as St Thomas', its well is said to have provided respite for pilgrims on their way to Beckett's shrine in Canterbury. Other rumours suggest it was a sheep-dip, a mill-grinder, even a steam-roller fallen from a road. In spring, Holywell is carpeted with wild, white garlic flowers, ramsons, poised over fresh green, lily-shaped leaves.

We are on our way back to the car. I stand for a second looking up at Sugar Loaf Hill. To one side of it, the Canterbury Road carves through the chalk escarpment, above, and behind us roars the A20 as it is about to carve it's way into Round Hill tunnel, its concrete stilts rising from the field impressive. Closest of all, is the A259 roaring also, but prettily, at the base of the Folkestone Downs, as it makes its way towards town and harbour.

This is a significant place. Go to higher ground it whispers. Before the sun sets. Take the significance there. And we can, because we've got the car, that very thing that's ruining the peace here!

And so we wind along the Downs past Castle Hill, Cherry Tree Gardens and Cheriton Hill, stop over the White Horse where sunbeams shoot from behind a cloud, past Peene where we turn left and park at our usual place beside Shearin Bungalow.

Dog is ecstatic to be here. It began when he was a puppy. We shared some moments of tussocked joy in the grass round the base of the skeleton hawthorn you can see rising into the sky. He runs to this place looking for a stick to play with. It amazes me he has such a memory of that moment four years ago. That each time we come back here his already unbounded spirits lift so. Be it denuded, this is his tree still. Our place on the ground.

Picture Our relief at reaching this dramatic summit of Down brimming with silence.

Nodding to the Numinous

Arpinge and Etchinghill, A & E. Accident and Emergency it may be on the terrifyingly fast road with no pedestrian consideration separating Arpinge from Etchinghill, but recently I've have been linking the two in better ways. Their scarps and coombes are conjoined by a beautiful deep valley running one into the other. Antidote and Elation I will call them instead.

It is a few days before Christmas and having just read writer Jeanette Winterson's idea that religious festivals are designed for Time outside Time, get on a bit of a high horse about how Christmas might also be seen as the elation of miracle. Spirit has taken on body. Word has been made Flesh. Amidst the superficiality of shopping is something else. Our deep love of matter is still there: our cherishing of family and friends, the body and flesh we love and protect.

But enough. People would get bored.

Though I've not done altogether. Bearing witness, the flesh of the long grass on the terracetted flanks of Arpinge between Christmas and New Year is numinous. It retains the browny gold of late summer. It's so spongy my daughter lies down on it stretching out like the hills, covering my coat she's wearing with with mud from worm mound muds. My son crouches down with his camera to catch the shapes before him. The scarp stretches down in huge sweeps, on across the flat to a blindingly bright sea and blue sky, while the flank of an opposite scarp, already in monumental shadow because of the low winter sun, looms out of darkness and hazy vapours that that hang over the ground.

Hillyans are mythical hill folk. That's us, often on the edge.

Sometimes, it's not gentle where the slopes begin, but cut sharply though with soft grass not rock, the undulating line as incisively visible as the contours on the map. We tumble down on short, bright green grass between the long brown, Dog preoccupied with chasing the stick thrown for him by my son instead of rabbits, gaunt, leafless hawthorns of winter bending over us, bare branches of storm-struck trees lying strewn beside our route before we land. Magical gnarled woods, a muddy brook gushing madly at the base of steep banks, bare-soiled but for the first sprinklings of bright green fern. We're at the bottom, no longer at an edge, more in the centre, no longer dropping but cushioned and abundant.

Amy Liptrot, writer on the Orkneys, speaks of craving sensation on the edge, in extremes, and wants 'to be more alive'. As if life were only on the edge. But it's at the centre too, deeply deep, deeply balanced, deeply filling with life, unless that's just the privilege of not being like Amy, battling addition, always extreme.

In any case, we're up through the Beeches' bare-branched wood, the dazzling winter sun again streaming low through the slim tree trunks, no carpets of bluebell or ramson, just one or two fronds again of bright green fern. At the top on Etchinghill, another shadowed monolith of scarp booms into vision behind back-lit hawthorns, transfigured (Wilhelm, 1931:17). On the ground, green grass streams with a million cobwebs, wild, filigree gossamer ribbons, trembling white from every direction as we move left or right across the sun. Down from Etchinghill escarpment. Up to Arpinge.

We break off from Teddar's Leas Road to cross the Down-top to the edge-ledge we started off on, the sun setting to the right of Summerhouse Hill. A mist covers the sea to obscurity, Dungeness seemingly to be a castle in the air with three ships floating by in a sky, not above but beneath it.

Note: Body of risen Christ at Easter. 'Traces' left by the transfigured person's experience in Chinese Taoism, that individual who'd sought the fixed pole in the flight of phenomena (Wilhelm, R., Jung, C.G. (1931). *The Secret of the Golden Flower, A Chinese Book of Life*. London and Henley, RKP).

Dog's Tree

I have a picture of Dog in the shadow of his tree where he came as a puppy and ran unbounded for the first time through luscious grass. Careering in crazy zig zags he'd come to sit beside me beside the tree before rushing off again into the freedom of long grass. Each time we come back here he does the same thing. It helps me remember how strong his emotional memory is and how we were linked at the very beginning in the delight of this place.

Arpinge Escarpment

Mandala Me

'Get off my land', comes the voice of someone from my mobile. And for a second, before I realise my caller is joking, I think, how does the farmer know my number, let alone know I'm here? Besides I'm near the legitimate path. I'd just texted this acquaintance to say I couldn't talk for long as I might be coming into a field full of cows or sheep at any moment, which is how he knew to make the joke, but now luckily reception is bad so our conversation is terminated and I can leave him and it behind.

Dog and I get into a sensual lollop through long, lush grass, into the sitting down by our dead little tree position, looking out over the bay, feeling the warmth of spring and the openness of it seeping into dulled senses. Everywhere is equilibrium. No-one to disturb that. A distant couple with their sheepdog look the other way, like us, over the bay, just gazing.

Dog spies a grazing fox that looks like a dog to begin with. It sniffles and snuffs in the long grass at the top of the scarp, a sloping side dropping away into the shadowed valley. Dog chases it with graceful speed, only it seems, in game, no fuss when it has gone.

Elation born of equilibrium, fuelled by these grand and familiar gradients, brings an unfettered sensation from out of here, not nowhere, of a Mandala Me. Imagine we are a pattern made of textures and dense biological design and this a statement about the part of ourselves that can't be taken away unless this landscape is, an 'I' place, hooking us to it and our own independence simultaneously.

As uncontrollable but in our grasp, these are a gentle version of the mountains we might dream of. Tonight, I go to Annapurna for a meal with my daughter. Anna: food, grain. Purna: full, complete and perfect.

Arpinge Base: Unhinged Arpinge

Driven by an idea of sand dunes emulated in a landscape without desert I leave behind the gravel track sheathed in shadow all the way to the base of a hill rising in the northwest, to climb the gate onto a flat land at the base of other hills. Following its wide and turfy route beside a line of trees to a bend in the coombe, roughly at the base of the spur, there they were. Sun-kissed flanks of the Downs rising brightly like golden sand dunes interspersed with lonesome notches of grass.

There was no burning fear of the desert's sun, but human-made facts of unease. MOD property. Was I unhinged by Arpinge, or was a tiny red plane really flying overhead, then another, black one, spying on me? I hadn't got sunstroke, this wasn't sizzlingly hot sun desert and there were no soldiers. And if Dog disturbed a pheasant or two and chased rabbits – without harming or hurting them – this was no conservation area with rules we might be breaking.

The unease was perhaps to do with the height, endurance and age that these imposing dunes possessed as they towered over us, we pinpricks but highly visible in the low openness of the coombe.

With the planes vanished there are no spies overhead so the unease that persists when we leave is probably more to do with the dunes' relative permanence against our ephemerality, monoliths of my psyche! Greater still is the imprint they leave here which, like a dream filled and risen to surface consciousness, leaves dents of bounteousness lasting until this day, their forms curving sinuously into a late afternoon amber sun taking up residence in my mind.

Barrow, Arpinge Escarpment

Just as fascinating ten months later, a day after the clocks had gone back, is the haunting beauty and loneliness of these deserted but majestic dune-like shapes. We didn't traverse the out of bounds/do not enter/Ministry of Defence fence but opened a legitimate gate and found the rather small and overgrown path that led through brambles and over another fence into the open field at Arpinge's base. On this evening's spurs, we were met with glorious, wholehearted, unsinister, unthreatening sunshine. Shadows arrowing into light.

Dog is rabbits-away, streaking up the golden terracetted flanks, and eventually I follow, emerging again and again from long shadows into sunshine, then away from the course we sometimes follow beside a trickle in a dampened creek, along a cow path traversing upwards, right up from base to the spur's summit, from darkness to light, from depth to height, till all before us are Brockman's Bushes and Summerhouse Hill on Arpinge's scarp with the Bay stretching right round and away making its semi-circle of sea. Then with this crazy allegory alight, we tumble down on the large soft totts of grass without twisting ankles or paws. Dog finds the best path for me, anxiously returning to make sure I can make it and, hey presto, we're back to our legitimate gate, geese cackling nearby.

Arpinge Escarpment

Seabrook Stream's Spring

Seabrook Stream's spring breaks out in a crevice between two of Arpinge's curvaceous spurs. Fifty-seven species of crane-flycranefly are said to be found in its burgeoning undergrowth which veils its deep opening into and out of the earth. Seabrook Stream ferments and foments out of an invisible chalk chasm, crashing then tinkling free of the scarp into this long and luscious coombe.

Fog

A huge pylon looms out of the mist, buzzing, not with the comfort of electricity it brings to our easy homes but strapped with 'danger of death' signs.

Going out in the fog alerts me to something about our relationship with nature. Being unable to see clearly into the distance might provoke fear or excitement, but also a little mischievous comfort. While we can't see others, nor can they see us.

This pylon so placed alerts me to the idea that fog hides something else too:, that nature, which provides so much solace and elation, can only abide within the knowledge that arms us when we go out on a cold winter's day, of a warm home with four walls to return to. The smell of dew on the grass or the damp mud might not feel so rejuvenating if we had to curl up this very night and sleep on it.

Still, for a second, I question as a falsely romantic notion, this rhythm of moving untouchable through these fresh places as a falsely romantic notion, relishing all the details of a civilisation I've come out here to lose, when tonight I will sleep in a warm bed with a roof over my head leaving the earth odours outside with the pylon relaying energy to us.

Peene, looking east

Peene

Keen for Peene in November

You bet. I've been pursuing Peene like a dream, and not only that, but a camera that works. This will be the third time I've come here and each time, apart from today (touch wood), the camera's jammed and blurred, the sharp sunshine marking out sharp shadows going unrecorded.

When I consider why this matters and what I'm am I after, three words slip incidentally to mind. Beauty. Articulacy. Belief. As if 'I' depended on my persistent pursuit of Peene, the recording of perception. Distilling essential moments. Keeping true to that 'moment Satan cannot find'.

Peene lies between the escarpments of Arpinge and the Folkestone Downs. Its North Downs Way path leads above Eurostar's sleek rail-tracks, towards the sea, to begin the end of its journey that begins in Farnham and rolls on its eastern stretch through Wye, Brabourne, Postling, Tolsford Hill and Arpinge characterised by chalk cliff, to Dover.

It was an old chalk limestone quarry for mortar and whitewash. Views from it look east, west, north and south and bright sunshine discloses deeply shadowed terracettes of the Downs and the evening haze around the old landmarks of Summerhouse Hill, once 'mound' hill, and Brockman's Bushes.

Peene Quarry

Folkestone Downs

Just East of Peene below the White Horse springs St Eanswythe's watercourse. She is Folkestone's patron saint who founded the first nunnery in Folkestone in 630, and grand-daughter of Ethelbert, the first Christian King of Kent, said to have welcomed St Augustine to our shores in 597.

Perhaps the strip of raised land from Arpinge to Peene constitutes the Folkestone Downs, but here they begin recognisably with Cheriton Down and Cherry Garden Hill leading to Castle, Round and Sugar Loaf Hill on Crete Road West, sliced from Crete Road East by the Canterbury Road. Wingate and Creteway Down run along Crete Road East to Dover Hill and the sea edge, then along the white cliffs to Walmer and Kingsdown to the east.

These are the landmarks that form the distinctive land mass which is characteristic of these Downs. No cliffs yet but coombe-fretted buttresses of open grassland whose lofty scarp ridges are topped with mounds, barrows and earthworks from different periods. Then, from the south of Castle Hill, not only can you look down over Folkestone to the sea and France beyond, but also get a clear view of Folkestone Downs' spine as it curves in and out as far as that other knob, Summerhouse Hill, not unlike Sugar Loaf.

The Downs' south facing slopes are balmy and continental in the summer, host not only to downland plants such as dwarf thistle, horseshoe vetch and squinancywort but also the spider orchid, usually more at home on the calcareous rocks of southern Europe. Flora includes annual rye grass, kidney vetch flowers fed on by the rare blue butterfly caterpillar, upright brome grass, oxeye daisy, fescue grass, quaking grass, birds foot trefoil, fed on by the common blue butterfly caterpillar, field scabies, selfheal, to name but a few.

To its east, linked by Horse Shoe bend and Round Hill is Sugar Loaf Hill. A thin, slippery, precipitous path leads over the top of the tunnel and the roaring traffic of the A20 that bores into Round Hill's terraced, grassy chalk slopes which heroically resist modernity's ferocity, but still it is nicer to take the steep but softer and more widely generous slope of Round Hill's shoulder. Then to pause a while to look over the dramatic cone which is Sugar Loaf Hill, terraces and ridges sharply defined by shadows on days when the sky behind it is bright and blue, or peppered, in early summer, with cowslips and orchids.

We don't have mounds of sloping sugar in our pantries anymore, and here the conical Sugar Loaf Hill, despite being reminiscent of Wiltshire's Silbury Hill, is no man-made artificial structure. Nor drumlin formed by glacial deposits. Neither was it always so pyramid-like. Once, presumably, it formed the end of a longer protuberance that became separated from the main hill by the erosion of waters slipping down its sides, and weather in general weathering. Now it rises from the width of its base-circumference to a point levelled by a tumulus in pleasing, softly rounded, neat shape, conspicuous to those arriving from over the sea. Just as Vortimer would have wished it [see piece on Sugar Loaf Hill].

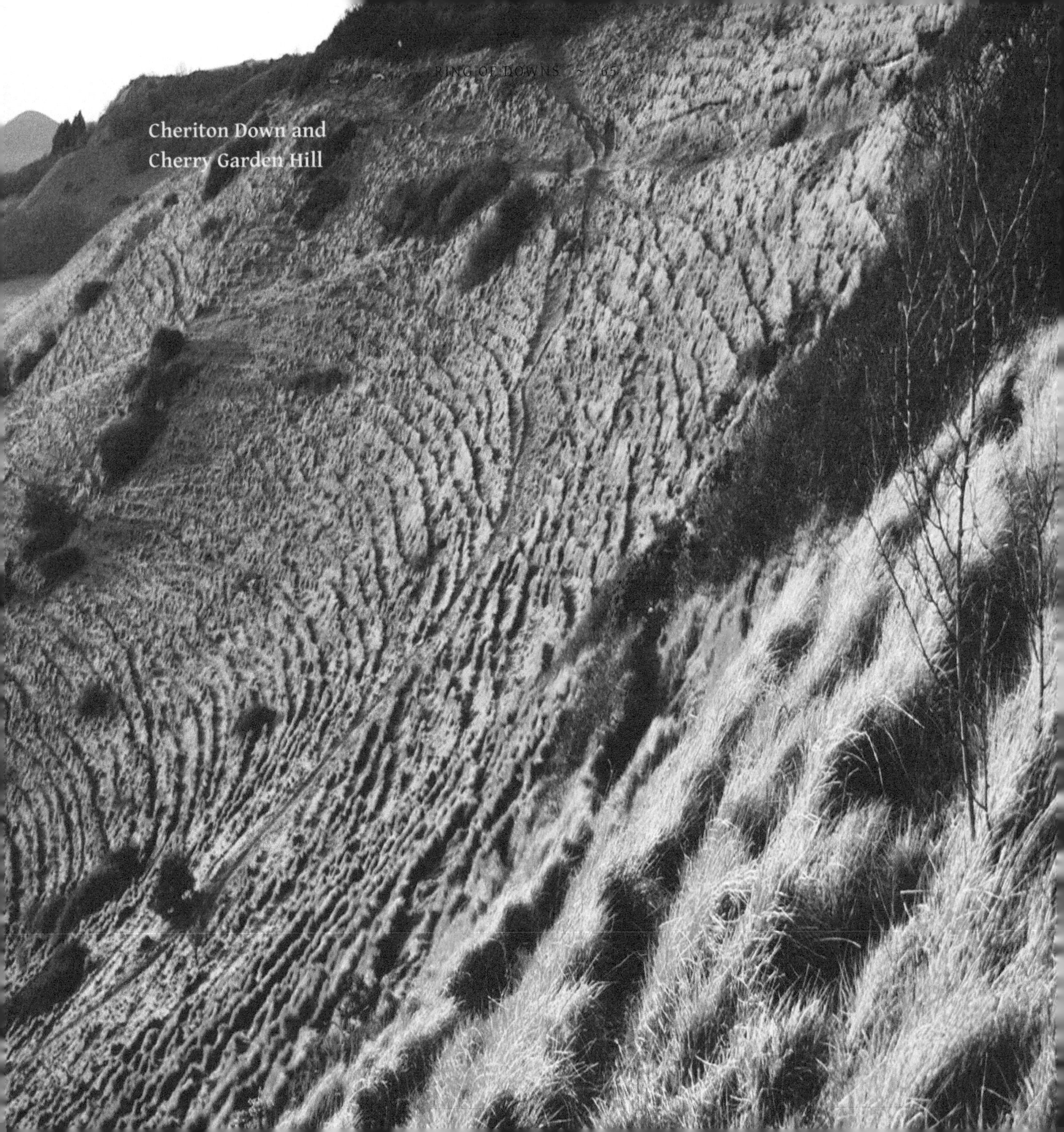

Cheriton Down and
Cherry Garden Hill

Balancing

Dog looks to be balanced precariously at the top of the flank while he stands on one leg to do a pee, but he's as steady as a rock. I'm the one that's hanging on, clinging to this Down's surface as if it were a rockface presiding over a crater, which if I were to fall into would be the Channel Tunnel Terminal.

A place of extremes. This must be one of the steepest Down scarps. The Terminal possesses an overwhelming eyeful of tracks. Here they are — extreme nature and extreme human construct — juxtaposed together. Not so much in an inbetween, liminal space as one of edgeness.

For up on our edge of delightful but ankle-twisting slopes, we are separated from the turmoil quite distinct from the rattle and clatter of colliding metal and squeak of brakes. So, I bring out my inner mountain goat, who treads happily and lightly along the furrowed ledges. Dog and I together as steady as a beating drum seeing out these long locomotives dragging immense lorries in serious snakelike procession towards Europe.

Castle Hill

Although Castle Hill is also known as Caesar's Camp, its origins aren't Roman, unless it was a Roman picnic site as Roman coins were found here. In fact, its ringwork and bailey was built by the Normans around 1140, a thousand years after the Romans. Some 800 years later a 'tank trap' ditch was dug during the 2nd World War II.

The modern footpath follows the route of the ancient, raised causeway used by the Normans. The ringwork of earth banks and ditches would have provided defence for the wooden castle, homes and a chapel. Within the ringwork was a bailey housing soldiers as well as storerooms, workshops and stables.

The only excavation took place in 1878 by General Pitt Rivers, the Victorian father of modern archaeology, when pottery and flints were found from the late Neolithic (Stone Age) period 4000 years ago. A chalk scar on the south bank was made by this dig. From hundreds, perhaps thousands of years of grazing, a flower-rich grassland has developed.

Washed and weathered. Weathered and washed. That was the walking, foot-stepping rhythm of the mantra picked up on the Warren's Apron from the water and wind of furrowed waves dancing and breaking on the rocks.

Washed by the sea.

Now weathered by the land. Motionless. No mantra.

Just absorption with the lens, photographing the soft undulating hills around Castle Hill, that appear, in a late evening light, like sand-dunes, covered by flattened winter grass, dry and light brown. With shadows here, the setting sun there, I play with shapes of a golden desert like the undulations of waves, trapped happily in a timelessness with 'no beginning or end'. Until thinking of the past brings back the present. If I am weathered here, so much more must have been the spurs, scarps and coombes of long ago, ferocious gales, rains and rivers pouring through the soft chalk hills to mould them into what we see now.

Sugar Loaf Hill

Sugar Loaf Hill

Sugar Loaf Hill and King Arthur

Legend has it that Vortimer wanted to lie where he could be seen, to remind the people that his spirit, at one with the earth, was here to stay, protecting the land from would-be invaders across the sea. Geoffrey of Monmouth describes a 'brazon barrow' that was to be built, and hence stories associating Sugar Loaf Hill with a mighty pyramid shaped tomb and Vortimer's burial might have been picked up by 19th century antiquarians. But Vortimer's wish was never fulfilled and Sugar Loaf is not man-made. Except, perhaps, for the ancient tumulus, burial mound, on top thought to have been built around 450-60 AD. Vortimer had been poisoned by Rowena, his father Vortigern's Saxon wife, as he didn't follow his father's support of the Saxons. Vortigern is said to have given mercenaries, headed by Hengist and Horsa, the Isle of Thanet as their base but later they turned against him.

It has been suggested that the legend of Vortimer, heroic leader who fought many a battle driving back the Saxons in the second half of the 5th century might be at the forefront of the Arthurian one: Arthur an amalgam of Vortimer, Ambrosius and Riothamus, other brave leaders of the time instrumental in driving back the 'barbarians'. Despite what we can or can't prove and believing perhaps that legend possesses an inkling of a truth that gives rise to it, something, however tiny, might have *occurred.* Besides, tapping local tradition into mainstream myth, like into the collective unconscious, makes the mic/mac analogy again between us and the world more tangible.

So, we now have Kent to add to the counties of Cornwall and Somerset fabled to tell something of the great King Arthur – whether his birthplace at Tintagel, Cornwall, or his victory at Bath/Badon, his court of Camelot in South Cadbury and his burial place at Glastonbury, all in Somerset. This lovely flow of hills, particularly Sugar Loaf, overlooking Folkestone, *Lapis Tituli* (inscribed stone) as it is depicted by antiquarian William Stukeley in 1725, might also have had an important role in the drama of Arthur. So, too, nearby Barham Downs, not just the scene of Caesar's defeat of the Briton's in 54BC or William I1's meeting with the Men of Kent in 1066, but said by Malory to be the place of Arthur and Mordred's penultimate battle.

But whether preoccupied by the emotional heights of myth, measurement, Easter or lark-song that Sugar Loaf Hill inspires, there's also much to be said for the wooded depths of these landmarks, tucked away at the foot of a scarp, as they turn away from the coast. At the base of Sugar Loaf Hill lies the tussocked Holywell Fen, one of the last in the area. And the lush, leafy hollows of Holywell Coombe where chalk rock meets gault clay, abounding in fresh-water springs. Small ravines with a myriad of streams and confluences pour out from under the rain-saturated hills, their soft earthy banks studded with badger sett entrances. Secluded wooded paths lead around the base of the hills and, were it not again for the roaring traffic of the M20 and A20, all this could be paradise.

Blip on Landscape

When I visit Sugar Loaf Hill where local folklore taps national myth, I am considerring how we may be no more than blips on the eternal unconscious of our ancestors. Humbling and elevating at the same time, leaving me today and now, here, scrambling up and down chalk escarpments with Dog. When he first came here, I slipped down a steep slippery chalk path and swore at him for not helping me. But, all this time later, he does. I'm slipping. Here Dog, I call, and he rushes back so I can get a grip of his collar and slowly, me balancing against him, we descend without my slipping. All these years later we share a language. We're going up here I say, and he goes up, we're turning left, and he turns left, then down, or right, whichever I say he's there before I am. Together a tiny blip of combined consciousness on a lilting landscape.

Holywell

In spring, Holywell is carpeted with the white flowers of wild garlic on fresh green, lily-shaped leaves, ransoms, and at its heart is the well once known as St Thomas'. Was it a resting place for pilgrims *en route* to Thomas Beckett's shrine in Canterbury or a sheep dip? Or is its round stone a mill-grinder, a steam-roller that fell from the motorway or one like the Holy Well of Glastonbury, used for cups to imbibe the sacrosanct and holy-healing stuff? These questions of the what and the how and the history and geology serve best as background to the here and now present, with us soaking it all up in sunshine or rain, whatever the weathering and reckoning of today.

Wingate Hill

The curving delineation of Wingate Hill's protruding spur hovers dramatically over the complimentarily bending roads of Folkestone's streets below. The sweep and curve of roads with modern houses turning this way and that, quite tidily, are offset by a tall viaduct and topped by a Martello tower on a green hill before the sea. A group of homes cling limpet like to its protective base after which the wing rises almost vertically. Wing Ate Hill.

In the area behind Dover and Wingate Hill a fog cloud is soft and translucent in this grey but glowing atmosphere, seagulling it wispily, unflappedly, over the Folkestone Downs and out across the Channel.

The green shoots that sprouting so keenly from a burnt sienna earth in autumn aren't the result of hand-planted labour but labour-saving machines. They stretch and spread over curves and dips so perfect in their exact lines, so natural yet manufactured, so 'artwork'. The sprouting green shoots look like stiches threaded with wool severed to make fluffy-feel cardigans. Or digitisation spreading over the surface of our land as filigree fine as this line of trees.

Dover Hill, Creteway Down

With the thought that landscapes are conduits to older mysteries, place itself weaving threads and drawing people in across time, I wander along the heights of Dover Hill.

How strategic it is in the bright, almost too clear August light that stretches over the water as far as the white cliffs in France. It also boasts the highest point in southern England along the coast after the Golden Cap further west in Dorset.The highest point on the whole Downs (not just on the coast) is actually a third of the height of England's highest peak, Scafell Pike in the Lake District. That is at Botley Hill in Surrey which is a Marilyn (150m).

But, it is most strategic here, because after having crawled all the way across land from Farnham, it is about to skirt along the coast, its chalk cliffs rising from Folkestone to Dover. Over the brow of Wingate Hill and Creteway Down it takes its last journey over inland. Or, looking at it the other way, it's turning here away from the sea to begin its long journey west.

Folkestone Museum houses evidence of an ancient heritage: a woman named Aefre, who along with graves of forty other Anglo-Saxon men, women and children, as well as broches, buckles, beads, weapons and pottery, was found in a cemetery at the base of Dover Hill in 1906. They had probably lived in a village further down towards Folkestone, the Kingdom of Kent being one of the first regions to be founded by Anglo-Saxons comprised of Germanic, Jute and Angle in 455AD.

Folcanston is the first mention of something resembling Folkestone, and this cemetery was in use when Augustine arrived in 597.

The Warren

The Warren

Between the sea and high chalk cliff lies the vegetated undercliff of the Warren. Split by the railway line, the Upper and Lower Warren lie to its north and south. The landslide which took the cliffs towards the sea is now covered by wood, scrub and grassland.

Dropping down on a steep path from the Upper Warren's high cliffs, home to the kestrel and peregrine falcon said to fly up to 180mph, I had the sense as I penetrated the thick woodland of the Lower Warren dappled with unearthly sunlight, that I was entering a Garden of Eden.This luxuriant short stretch of forest sandwiched between cliff and shore with its own microclimate feels on a humid day to be like a tropical rainforest jungle. Its lush vegetation is full of lichens, moss and creeper ropes of *Wild Clematis* that climb the scrub to form a canopy (covered in the autumn by the downy seeds of *Old Man's Beard),* dangling over muddy moist coombes and massive clumps of bright green under further canopies of high soaring trees thrown into extravagant gestures.

This place is an idyll of small, secret streams and ponds that have formed in dips, cracks and broken ravines surrounded by a luxuriant undergrowth of grasses, wild flowers and orchids such as the *Pyramidal, Bee, Lady, Common-spotted* or *Late Spider.* Dragonflies and butterflies, attracted by the nectar-rich, garden escapee, Buddleia, fill the air. Patches of velvet turf are invaded by thorny hawthorn and blackthorn bushes and a woodland carpet of *Hart's Tongue Ferns* and *Horsetails* that give the whole a particularly primeval feel. Wild irises, primroses and white blossoms of wild cherry and hawthorn herald spring.

Looking out from the trees, I spy the beach and gently lapping waves, idyllic too, as if I were emerging from jungle to the edge of a desert island. On the flat under the chalk cliffs, I might look back up or beside me to see the rare delicate *Rock Sea Lavender, Wild Cabbage* and *Rock Samphire.*

Further down in the Lower Warren a variety of diverse plants, often whipped by salt-laden winds, nestle perched on crumbling white ledges. I am reminded that in the winter the jungle may be a wilderness of thorn and bramble and here of slippery, tumbling clay and rock.

This wild, underdeveloped shoreline, the Warren, once covering what was a river valley, is ancient. In the 1950's, a sword was discovered in its sea, like ones in Weymouth, Dorset, and the Thames, dating back to 700 BC at a time when it was common to throw swords into the water, as with King Arthur, as a votive offering. Then the oldest sea-faring boat, some 3,500 years old, was found in Dover and is now on show, reconstructed from its parts, at the Dover Museum.

The Apron

The concrete part of the Warren is called the Apron and was built by British Rail between 1948 and 1953 as a 'toe weight' to hold back the forward movement of the cliffs and protect the track that had been built through the Warren in the 1840's. From it, in 1979, the first man-powered aircraft pedalled by Bryan Allen and designed by Paul MacCready made it across the Channel, and onto it, in 1987, the car ferry, the *Hengist,* was blown by heavy storms.

Edge Place

A bright, invigorating day caught
between sun and shade.
A dizzying frenzy of energy
between wave-slapped shore
and towering cliff.
Spirals of air quicken and glide
in shapes flaplessly winged out by seagulls
exhilarated at a centre
within this edge place funnel-of-breath

No Broken Hearts

Speaking loudly over paltry utterances,
the sea-scape weathers over broken hearts
like the rhythmic but irregular pounding
of the waves upon the shore
and the sparkling eddies of spritely shifting surfaces say,
there are no broken hearts,
the brightly blowing wind has whisked them quite away.

Black on White

On a warm, grey sultry day I took some particularly sad, disquieting thoughts that wouldn't leave me alone, to the Warren. A granite sky blended with a granite turquoise, gently undulating sea. Slurp and thud. Slurp and thud went the waves against the concrete Apron. While my footsteps, interspersed with a kick of Dog's pebble, first from my right, then from my left foot, built up a rhythm, a mantra in my mind began to form and take my fragile thoughts away — BLAH! —like the blazing cliffs still white against the grumbling grey. Through one white cliff bedazzling the grey came a rumble and distant roar of the high-speed train entering the tunnel into the cliffs.

I sat on a wall. Exasperated that his pebble wouldn't move now that I was stationary, Dog trotted to the edge of the concrete and stood still too, looking out to sea. Some way away from him sat a solitary fisherman on a rock. Who was duplicating who, and apart from confirming our symbiotic relationship, who knew what our crazy game meant? Still, it was as imperative as my fascination for the landscape and its history, our history - how many million years does this place stretch back? — but now Dog and I were both engrossed.

While I sat, his pebble lay beside me, but as soon as I made a move to rise, he'd scooped it up in a flash then run a little distance to deposit it gently in front of me to kick again.

When I obliged, it was with a fierce thwack that landed the pebble into a thick clump of valerium, and I thought that that would be the end of that. Not so. Dog stuck his snout into the bosky thicket and appeared triumphantly holding it between his teeth as delicately as if it were a raw egg. If you think I'm supposed to retrieve my demandingly disquieting thoughts you're wrong, I told him, as if he'd be interested, and resuming my triumphant kick of the pebble, cast those nasty intrusions quite away.

Grey: Why Does the Warren Water Move?

Why do the grey waters move
on a grey day without meaning?
The beast run,
the wind blow,
the waters roar?
It makes no difference answer or none.
Poised on the not here and now of the here.
Of the deeper darker dig
Denounced.
Taking in the beauty of the running beast,
the blowing wind,
the roaring waters,
the flesh and blood.
Liberated.

Trouble Over

It's not until I see a white feather blown along the surface of the concrete Apron under the towering white cliffs, smells of sweet manure blowing in this same wind, presumably from Capel, that I realise like the BLAH of my first Warren piece, my troubles have been blown, or kicked, as in the case of Dog's pebble, quite away. Under this vast impersonal white that repeatedly takes me out of myself I'm also taken in. A white cliff and feather-fold away from the hand that threatened to throttle me an hour ago, now dropped to an arm hanging loosely down its side. The in and out movement linking my breath to outside air not broken after all. And later the white cliff veiled by the shadow of night spreading the might of the sun's mind set.

Tempest

The Warren is always invigorating.On the edge. Telling it how it is. White chalk scribbled onto its concrete says, '*I have loved in the Warren. Twice.*'

Sometimes it is brutal and brutalist. The perishing wind whips and wipes over the ground and in-between the bare branches of the shrubs till the friendship it has slashed has becomes raw.

I saw your warmth and tolerance crack here as we walked along the concrete as if it were made of the hard stuff, you talking briskly, dismissively about a woman who irritated you.

A 'mad' man you did not see balanced on the edge of the concrete, toppling in slow motion, not doing Tai Chi but testing his sanity against an invisible air, leaning precariously against the wind he thought might hold him. I watched to make sure it did before turning back to listen to your admonishment of someone far away.

Yours was not the only friendship that this wind has slashed in the last few months leaving us feeling stark. We still have A, the second letter of our names in common. But that's all. DAvid and MAryanne with MAndy, MArcella. Da, Ma, Ma, Ma and Ka! Kali's destructive regress before progress. The brutal tempest.

Turned now into a not unhappy splash.

Washed and Weathered

On a freezing cold, sharp blue-sky day I have plans to go inland to the hinterlands of dry valleys, but we are driving up Wear Bay Road and the cliffs are standing out, brightly lit monoliths that cannot be ignored. Dog also has a particular feeling for these cliffs and the Warren, only on our way to this spot does he whine to get out of the car. So, we change our plans about the hinterlands, and head down to the Warren.

Good decision. The smashing too-quick-to-capture waves splinter against the rocks, having run the gauntlet along the shore's edge, hollow tubes furrowing sideways in a kind of ballet till they split forever on rock or jutting side of the Apron. Washed and weathered, that's the mantra, that's how we're treated, like everything else on this wild, windy, rugged stretch of beauty. Again I fall under its perfect spell, the continual sound of the smash and the crash of the washing waves, as well as my own focus in trying to freeze the moment, click after click, into the eye of the separating spray. Despite the cold consumed and involved with the wash and the weather. Dog's wet pebble shines in the setting sun beside the glaring chalk-faced cliffs.

To be at one with the continual churning in air of wave and wind that whipping and whirling at the edge that was once, some billion years ago, no edge, but united with the European edge now over the Channel, is to be whipped and whirled into an energy sunk into us. And be one again. Yet with big white bodies of chalk cliff prouder and stronger than the need to stay together, no choice between Remain or Brexit, humanity or separation, they've still made one – a choice – and still the enormous white bodies of chalk-cliff lunge as proud and strong as the longing for the once oneness with Europe.

The dull thud of water into a rocky hollow. The patter of droplets sprayed onto the concrete. The slurp and trickle of jaunty waves rippling, not too feistily, but with continuous, melodious sound. Chalk-cliff sliced sides. Stretched sea floor. France, sharp in the distance, dipping away. Dog with quivering jaw extracts his pebble from a crack in the concrete and carries it tenderly to safety.

Slithering Pool

On a track between and parallel to the Warren seafront and high cliff, my tired, anti-mind sense of churlishness is challenged by the soft susurration of the wind blowing through buddleia bushes. It is the cue for a whoosh that lies beyond what we see, but is embedded in it, to unravel from that force outside me, into my no longer flat self. The churning white waves, along the edge of a deep turquoise sea, might be a design along the edge of a fan, except that they are so lively, I can only be sucked into this wild and windy skip and dance by an air which is invigorating but warm, the sun caressing my bare brown arms and legs.

A lot of talk about how we are on holiday. But it seems so. The Warren beach looks and feels like a desert island. I would be loathe to leave here as much as I would loathe to be without sea, sun and sky. A little taverna along the beach might be welcomed, but more so this deserted expanse, even in high season August. In the distance, I can hear holidaying families screaming and laughing in the waves. Their exultation in the wind infects us all.

A thinly moving pool of wave-end slithers across the concrete Apron. I am fascinated by the control with which an energy coming in the wind from such a distant sea, draws to conclusion. A huge weight that turns to feather. By a tide which not only pulls us out but also causes this tremendous force to halt as if someone had put on the brakes, just by my feet. That's enough thank you...stop...and it goes no further.

My tiny in time mind recaps, even if inaccurately, that the Greensand or Kent Ragstone was formed in shallow waters about 120 million years ago. Gault clay as the sea got deeper about 110 million years and chalk formed from microscopic algae, coccoliths, about 90 million years ago.

The Sea

Folkestone

Sea Saw Sea

For three nights the moon had looked full,
the skies clear,
a silvery light had haunted the ripples of the sea
streaking out behind a silhouetted tree.
But the seasaw place that leaves us rolling
Between what is vulnerable
And what resilient
Without abiding in either,
Will, if we've the stomach for it
Bounce us up and down
Like boisterous children on their sea-saw
From strength to weakness
And back again.
So the nights that were clear turn foggy, the smell of fog mixing with the briny sea it now hides,
and the night that was cold before brings a warm air the next day
with differences spewed forth by the changing winds from this seasaw sea
that bends trees and grasses and wobbles the shrubs that shake in it,
jelly on a plate, then sends a warm, gentle, misty breeze that is alleviating.
And when the sunlight eases through the mist to reveal,
Ever so surreptitiously,
a visible horizon with azure pools of light crossing the swishing, slurping sea,
and a benign wind whispers again through the whispering trees,
our spirits rise in amazed whisperings too.

Dog Days

Dog days aren't tired but happy ones
That course with life and light
And canter with energy in eternal delight.
Waves slash through jolting winds a-sail
Black dog ripples nose down
Headlong into the howling gale
Wind in the sea spray, wind in the wind, snout in the grass
Rippling sea-surfaced, sleek-furred, black dog
Trots the promenade, crunches the shingle
Come wind-blow wave-lash
Streaking along beside me.

Dog Slant

Straight as a die the dog walks,
the thought talks,
shining blindingly off the sea the sun pierces through branches,
preserving against all evil
that 'moment Satan cannot find',
talking and walking at a slant,
rippling dog purpose.

Mermaid Beach pier

Sure Line

The shore is a changing line,
an invisible limit that stops the sea from covering the land,
that stops me, just, from becoming a part of its eternity,
sending the chucking waves back to where they came from,
leaving me sorely solid and longing
but astonished on the shingled seashore.
Don't tantalise, take me with you, I plead.
But the blue sky, so much more dissolved than I,
looks laughingly down.
Blue light has a shorter wavelength than other colours I am told
and is therefore more likely to scatter.
I am not scattered like the blue but held here, fast,
in the longer, richer waves of the sunset's oranges and reds
that shiver with intensity.

Sea Snippets

March

When the fog is low and the sight is poor and the night is dark, the waves are loud. And I tumble more unsteadily than a pack of cards, upright in this enchanted mist-covered night, lauding it playfully over the indefatigable sea.

April

The shingle as flood prevention has been fashioned by machines into rising ups and sinking downs. The waves lap gently, in and out, in and out. The sun behind clouds flashes laps, in and out. All is in destabilising movement on which we're awash but not fallen.

June

Were the night not filled with anxieties, the morning could be a tabula rasa. As it is, the tabula rasa can be laid, artificially, anxieties being driven away. Ah, all is clear. I am inside brick. And, when I open the window, I can hear the wind in the trees and in the waves, and when I walk over the grass and down the cliff, I am beside the blowing blustering sea, waiting for me, bouncing and turbulent clear.

July

As the sky is clear, the darker patches in the pattern over the evening sea can't be cast by clouds, but breezes. Ever so slightly they ruffle the surface against the lighter streams that seem to run like rivers around these shadowy sea-breeze islands.

Moon Shine

It's not fairy lights that flicker in the branches of the fir tree on the undercliff, but something more alive, flickering relentlessly, heaving to and fro against but behind its big, wide sweeping branches. What is heaving to and fro is upon the water in the dark behind the tree. The moon. Upon the sea it shines and its beams dance, showing themselves only partially as fairy lights behind and upon the tree, before moving out away from its silhouette, onto the sea in an expansive, full-moon shine.

Pinch and Rise

Every now and again, I have to pinch myself when I look out at the sea which wraps itself like velvet dreams around my home, visible from most windows, no explanation needed.

The unquenchable vastness that plays with me a tiny pinprick on its ebbing and retreating story as unfathomably as a universe I can only imagine, is best described by me as eternity. And its promise. It haunts both conscious and unconscious mind.

Over the edge but not threateningly, it tips me gently into dreamland, so much more capable than I, lacing its arrival with soft, perfectly white foam that spreads across pebbles like rough bread rising, and gathers it up again in deep tinkling gurgles. I'm sucked up enchanted and popped back come south westerly or northern wind.

And, when the north wind doth blow and we shall have snow, a crimson sun unseen all day, until now, is lowered upon a hammocked grey cloud in this grey wintery light from under another dark granite cloud, plop, not into the sea, but somewhere behind it, sinking to rise so low I feel I can feel it in my body.

Portal

My daughter whose name is a palindrome, readable both ways, has brought me down to forage for mussels in the shallow pools, showing me places matching her brightness that can be read both ways too, but one revealing what the other has left out, low tide the other end to high.

So, I know there's a portal between concrete coastal path and rocky, low-tide shore, the littoral that speaks for humans to justify their lives and makes me wonder why I'd want to travel when everything I love in land and seascape is right here. It would be greedy and I haven't even got to the portal's opening yet.

Sure enough, once off the concrete, beyond the shingle onto the sand and rocks left by low tide that new world opens. Dog initiates it with a large round pebble, hard to get a grip on. It slips easily out of his mouth and has to be retrieved by digging. It is this, partly, that stops us from having a speedy walk and lands us instead in a slow but gushing world inhabited by water. The gentle rippling sounds of the slight waves, the bubbling up of water through holes in the sand. The tinkle trickle of the retreating tide. It is a sweet-sounding cacophony as overtaking as dancing clouds' blotting between the spark and shatter of a shifting sun.

We see in the shapes of running waters on sand huge vistas of mountain ranges and land formations. Cormorants, gulls and slabs of humanly-placed concrete creeping with dark seaweed silhouette on the horizon, though placed on the edge of a single history on ancient exploded and eroded rock, feel a long way from humanly deposited shingle. Walking on other days, along the concrete promenade looking out over the changing sunlight and El Greco clouds or a horizon turned into a streak of golden orange is extraordinary but walking this morning on the seabed is to be touched in helpless relation to Other.

The world from the esplanade is filled too with the magic of space in sea and air that breathes healing into the soul. And carries it like the arching, from exquisite flatness, of a small, white-crested wave breaking, very softly, on the shore, leaving more flatness behind it on which to float. Float I would, day by day, on its glistening surface. Then sail. Were it not now that I see three Russian warships sail by – not 'come sailing in' – and know they're not for Christ's Mass.

Seafront Son

Bold creature in rapture
Wrapped enfolded
In my arms.
Gentle baby spilling laughter
Thirty years ago.
Thirty years old.
Walking by the sea.

Lines of softness
Collude and calcifiy
Into hard-edged islands
Waves breaking and repeating
Through inlets they've made
Shine-feasted maleable
Breaking and repeating
Still.
The moaning unravelling wave
Never heeding the lines
Mounts its crest to break and unfurl
Smashing with unlined spume
Breaking matter
Mater-nally
Breaking through.

Storm Blasted

Ravished, exhausted and bludgeoned in blasts of light by churned-up spumey stormwaters heaving hydro power. For two nights, the wind has crashed and smashed against our doors in frantic, impolite knockings. For two nights, we have been pounded.

On the promenade, light tamarisk branches have been dissected in small strips, torn off from their first notches, and splayed into a corner where concrete sea wall meets concrete promenade. Happy now, a softly cushioning fuzz, and above that where water has poured down the walls from a sea-flowing stream, they have stuck, like a carpeted green wall. Further up the path, a tree blazes in the sun.

One Evening

Nearing 4 o'clock, late for the light from a mid-winter's day, the sea is as silky smooth as a lake. Silkies, a man might have told me, have been spotted between this stretch of seafront at Sandgate and the groin protruding at the turning point towards Folkestone. Only he doesn't say silkie or selkie – they haven't been walking on land – he says, seals. A fisherman has seen two playing in the waters.

Patches of water, some frisked up very gently by a tiny almost unfelt breeze, shift the surface in-between the pure glassy areas. I am mesmerized as by a dream — and I've had plenty of those featuring sea since the beginning of the year — by extreme sun in strong sky blue on navy sea matched by pure, clear, white linen on my symbolic bed. These winter days of low, intense sunshine are a knock-out.

I will sit on the beach with Dog to watch the sun go down and see if we can spot the seals. Granite grey, metallic waters shift under the blue to peach, to orange, to apricot even paprika-speckled contrailed sky. No seals. But a pair of cormorants turned toward each other on the deeply ribbed and glistening ripples, like a stately king and queen.

That night in my dream the huge golden orb of sun sets again, sinking into shards of peach that trickle and spurt along a fading horizon. And there to the left in the water below where the cormorants were, a seal head pops out, then another, and another and then one more, until there are four.

Harbour Arm

When I am tired and feel like giving up, I remember I am living by the sea. The sea will see me sleep. It will embed me. I will go to bed.

And after I will get up and ride along the littoral, silver-backed sharp clouds black in the distance above and against a blue sky, glorious as the bluebells in the woods. Dog runs along beside my bicycle, fur from his tail, ears and legs funnelled in the wind. The wind and the ride and the sun is on our side as we arrive at the entrance to the Harbour Arm.

The swing of harbour and Warren line flick in and out of shadow and light. Low jazz and funk tunes play as we walk, 'quiet dreams, a quiet thought, a walk alongside running streams', pre-empt the ooze of hotter days, and all suggest, 'why fuss?'

This is the dust we were and the dust we are, the sea our death and our life so far. This is the life on the Harbour Arm looking over the sharp light over the sea and the cliffs and the tables. This is the life. From a brick and concrete peninsular leading to a lighthouse at sea, we look back to harbour, beach and cliff. Dog befriends a man's food while I see the shapes in nature and in the skyline as the shapes of my voice.

Goodbye Ball

The day I met the beach-hut caretaker on the beach, the wind and waves were high, but not yet so high, he said, that the still in-coming tide would not cover the promenade in pebbles, loud fierce waves propelling them there with the same almighty force as the wind keeping me awake the night before.

Sure enough, two days later, we tread the promenade now covered in stones by a ferocious tempest as if it were shingle.

That morning the dog's ball has been peed on, but the now gentle waves have washed it clean and spilled into my shoes with the discomfort too of wet socks, and although Dog has been lifting it from the water's surface without getting too wet, it now takes its turn into tragedy or new life.

For away from the little waves carrying the ball back to the shore, it has reached the point of no return. It has just popped over onto the other side of this wave and now bobs, pitifully, always out of our reach. The paradox is: it's on its way out to sea even though the tide is coming in. 'Goodbye ball', I say, treating Dog who won't swim in the sea like a toddler.

Dover

Roll over to Dover

A monotone grey day in Dover on green and blue of grass, sea and sky. All grey except the white chalk track, damp in the vapour cast by mist hanging and dragging in the air. All grey, despite the dramatic plunge of cliff to rock far down below, the grey-white horses rushing in. All grey, except the almost glowing of the white track back from the turf, and scrubland of scampering white-bobbed rabbits running away from Dog. All grey, except that now it is almost dark, it is almost black, and looking down on the bright lights of the port, the gloomy grey is cast away.

This is Dover but we might be in the South of France; an electric twilight-lit Monte Carlo, multi-mono toned.

Beyond Dover; Kingsdown Beach

A mackerel sky above chalk ground saddles a shoreline suffused by a myriad tones of blue-greys and whites in a lifting bright light. We're ushered in to its inbetween but expansive world to look out and wide as we crunch the shingle, release Dog's ball into mellow, unfurling waves.

The chalk cliff rises towards St. Margaret's at the end of Kingsdown Beach. We walk *now* on chalk that has been pushed up by fault lines aeons ago. Like treading on a glacier this is a geology that can have you stopping in your tracks. Its surface bubbling, hard, but looking like the soft froth of fanning waves, impressive and memorable in the here and now but re-minding also that this chalk, laced with further aggregates of transforming rocks both above and below its own ground, flows on through other earths and under other seas, never even partially contained by our little Ring of Downs.

~ 4 ~

THE NORTH EASTERN ARC

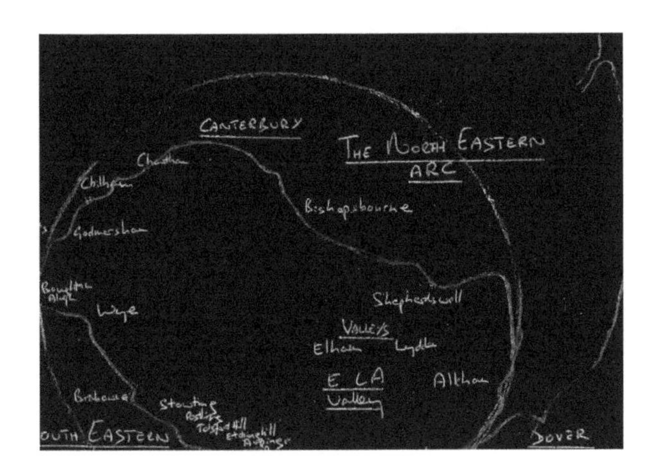

Boughton Aluph, King's Woods

Towards Canterbury

River Stour

North Downs Way
Farnham 98 miles
25 miles
Downs Way
30 miles

Boughton Aluph

Splitting Point

A Round becomes Whole

Here, where the eastern side of the North Downs divides, one part stretching north from west to east through Canterbury towards Dover, the other going south through Wye and the Folkestone Downs to Dover, lies Boughton Aluph. A criss-cross of tracks obfuscates the point where the North Downs Way actually splits at the west side of a round that will become my whole. A circle that will become my mandala.

I had expected raised downland to lead from one side of the Way's V then turn, still raised, to its almost right-angled brother, but the connection is more of a gentle, lowly, undulation of chalk-speckled, golden-cropped fields flowing into each other than dramas of scarps and coombes. Yet the Downs that I know can be seen from here on the Down hill behind Wye.

An extraordinary line of birds forms a V then a line, then another V with one side short, cutting through the distance like a wind-blown ribbon winding and unwinding from one formation into another, while we, beyond a big field,wind upwards on a tree-lined path into King's Wood's magic of silver-birch, and down again through beech woods, Boughton meaning 'of beeches'.

The West is the Best

Coming to this most western point of my ring almost flippantly as an 'on the spur of the moment' decision, was also of great significance. So great, in fact, that I refused to think of it or discuss it with myself because west is as simple as the setting sun, and I was dwelling on the pivot or conjoin between north and south. Nothing more be said or thought. Until words and thoughts sprang into life.

That the two sides going northeast and southeast from here, which have been seen to be marked by the way of the spirit and the way of the flesh, are here conjoined. Yet it was as if the conjoin itself, that there always had to be two sides to a thing, was preventing my unity and peace of mind, while I considered in typical First World anxiety how my car parked at Perry Court Farm would be trapped if the gates closed at going home time before I returned.

So there they were. The contraries that courted conjoin. Like freedom with fear. Green grass with bramble. Eternity with time. Held before me on this western plate. But how lucky. Eternity without time was endless, whereas here, now, my endlessness was restricted by worry, flesh feeling its own presence in each moment.

Perhaps my liberation was dependent upon the freedom to feel the fear cast by darkness that clouded vision. The fast road we'd just crossed. The slow death. The evil in men and women. Their inactivity. The farcical leaders. At north and south I was looking at the spirit and the flesh, the good and the evil, the grass and the brambles, the eternity and the time, the freedom and the fear.

And lost them all again when Dog's lead went missing, but had the symbol of that neatly impressed upon me. That while this instrument of restraint was no more, so in tune were we with each other it was unnecessary, and we would be free in our moments of eternity, release, heavenly grass. Despite the car on the other side of the road. That this once soft summer grass is now September's brittle stubble of harvested lines on many of these fields that hanging around the western gate confirms it. Somehow. In the flatness not the height.

And where I've had a comfort stop, I'm comforted to claim a detective memory in retracing my steps back to it. The lead I do not need is buried in the lush grass where I stopped after all. A liminal world at west between north and south and lost and found. A liminal place too for the North Downs, where not only does it split to go north and south but leaves the straightness it started near Farnham that continuesd for miles as a single, linear trackway balanced often half way down the slope, going east, to become a circle. At which point this typical Down landscape changes into something else as it begins to roll distinctively and impressively into scarps and coombes. At least on the lower, fleshier, southern loop of the circle. Of the other northern loop, I know less well, despite myself and studies of spirituality. Now, this September 2017, is the time to start. On the northern arc that keeps the vision.

King's Wood

Reclining Body

I skirt the edge of King's Wood as if I were tracing my lover's skin and we were on high looking down at a valley beyond which are hills caught in the orange glare of sun-down. At this most westerly point where the straight-ish North Downs Way divides to go north and south, the up of the Down — which rises to Wye Downs at the start of the southern section and King's Wood starting the northern — dips. And here I lay my body down, metaphorically, momentarily.

There is something open and glorious about the Stour Valley, low enough to catch the extraordinary light of flat and marshlands with signs of hill rising out of it in a still low distance, which once , when you get into, rolls like warm flesh as if landscape has substituted lovers or they had entered into the land!

Toward Canterbury

Julieberrie

From King's Wood to Chilham and Julieberrie Long Barrow is a little detour away from the village on the banks of the Great Stour. Long Barrows are usually chambered tombs but Julieberrie is unchambered and was probably constructed in the Early Neo-lithic period 5th to 4th century BCE

Bigbury Iron Age Hillfort

It sounds as if water is running somewhere under the trees, but we're already quite high on the hill, so it's hard to understand where it's coming from. It's as perpetual as the breeze, which is what it turns out to be. Not water at all but wind. Not water but beech leaves lifted over the earth by a churning air which appear at first to be moths or butterflies fluttering just above the ground. Contrary to the water they sound like these light brown beech leaves are crinkly, crispy and dry.

Bigbury Camp, is the woodiest Iron Age hill fort I've been to, and feels a little unique in this respect, but also a little forgotten, even if human hands have piled sticks and shrubbery in neat sections upon the centre circle's bracken, and the smaller paths, with pernicious stems of thorny bramble ripping through my trousers and flesh, are impassable.

I know nothing about its history so it's a surprise to find that Caesar is believed to have fought his first battle with the Ancient Britons on English soil here in 55 BC. Previously it had been occupied by the Belgic people. It's described as a 'univallate' hillfort. That is 'having one raised edge, wall, rampart surrounding a depression'. To the north it has an enclosure, possibly a cattle compound, and archaeological digs have unearthed remains of a chariot and slave chains.

That this ancient woodland is to be maintained as a nature reserve explains its half-tendedness and presence of neat wood piles, and is the sound of running water a Roman haunting?

The River Stour

The Stour Valley, West Canterbury

The Valley of the Stour north of Wye is said to have been long been appreciated for its beauty as it flows towards Canterbury. In as much as I am no historian or geologist, nor am I much good at map reading apparently, how come it's taken me so long to find the River Stour's route into Canterbury? Halfway down Canterbury's High Street is a little bit of the river with tourist rides being offered, but no sign of a path beside. We've plundered the river in Godmersham and Olantigh with some beautiful results. We've strode across fields to walk only a short time beside it, some miles distant below Wye, for example, and the day before, along a pretty lane under Bigbury Castle woods, just after Harbledown we found it, and crossing a wooden bridge found Thannington, a residential area, where I could park next time.

Next time was July, about four years after I'd thought about wanting to find this river's entrance into Canterbury. One mile and a half into Canterbury, it says, but it feels more like two, a pleasant stroll, the beautiful bright green Ophelia-type reeds in the river being the most pleasing sight. On the way back Dog gets just out of his depth by mistake and swims. This is the first time he's swum in four years I note. Which just about sums things up. I've hardly chuckled at myself for viewing this information with such seriousness. I mean he's 'only' a dog. I haven't noted the last time I swam!

~ 5 ~

THE ELA VALLEYS

Elham, Lydden, Alkham

St Radigund's Abbey, Church Hougham, Farthing Common

Down Bluebell Woods

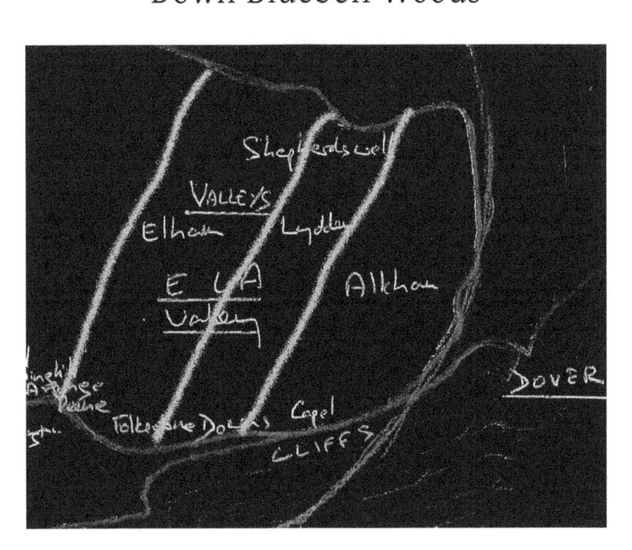

Elham Valley

Court at Denton, Elham East

I've just talked to my daughter who is off to Berlin, Krakow, Tatri Mountains, Slovakia and Vienna, and laughing at herself for having made such a tight itinerary of her schedule. Ella is her middle name and although only with one 'L' the sequence of the Downs' valley stretching inland from Folkestone, Elham, Lydden and Alkham, spells Ela, so I'll never forget it.

Denton is a valley between Elham and Lydden. We walk away from Denton Court with its church, St. Mary Magdalene along the side of a field with ripe, golden corn that stretches to the valley bottom, then up the other side, feeling exhilarated by this July abundance.

But on the other side of exhilaration grows a certain dread. From under our feet a pheasant squawks out of the corn, frightening me but exciting Dog. When we pass up into some woods a single pheasant startles us again, rising up in a screeching panic. Now there are not just one or two pheasants, but tens and even hundreds, some fledgings and the other larger ones coloured with beautiful feathers, flying up around us, with not just the smell of birdfeed and guano unpleasant but also the thought of their being bred for the kill. Ever more bird houses open up on our path, out through the woods and across another field, the creatures rising up in multiplying numbers like *The Birds* and getting louder. Some vanish into the creepy woods with buckets of food to make the killing better, and fences that wouldn't make any difference even if the birds did know how to escape.

But back by the Court and into the beautiful church the feelings of exhilaration turned to fear have been returned again to an exquisite vision anticipated by sumptuous cornfields: stained glass and the sun's reflection of it upon the wall.

Barham Down

If most open spaces breath freedom into the mind, others like Barham Down hang heavy. Maybe because of the talk of the battles here when Ceasar defeated the Britons, in 54 BC, and the 'Golden Calf' got buried in 56 AD when they were being driven back by the Roman soldiers and might still, it is said, be lying deep under the ground. Or that Arthur and Mordred. according to Malory, fought their penultimate battle here. Or that in 1066 William, who'd conquered, met the Men of Kent?

In the late nineteenth century, the Reverend Richard Harris Barham writing *The Ingoldsby Legends* used Tappington Hall Farm near Denton as the backdrop for the legend of the spirits of two brothers, a royalist and Cromwellian, who haunted it, and his *Witches Frolic,* set in St. John's Commandery near Swingfield, captures the mysterious beauty of a countryside infused with magic.

Then highwayman Black Robin frequented the slopes of Barham Down, terrorising travellers on the road and lanes round about in his black mask. The *Black Robin* public-house was his hide-out.

But delighted with this openness of space, Black Dog trots and sniffs along the path, scuttles and sniffs, poises balletically, one leg raised on the edge of a sniff, and focusing his snout upon the thicket, slinks closer to the ground before darting off after a squirrel. The oppression I feel might have nothing to do with these things after all. It might be connected with the perishingly cold March wind, the grey sky, the lift of hill that glides but never seems to quite take off, the sheer loneliness of it all in a sweeping, low statement.

Yet there's something almost hallucinogenic about its surface, so clear I need not be confused by the possibility of getting lost, yet find in this very deceptive distance a quality that disorientates: you expect to be able to turn around and see where you've been walking but thehat track has sunk ever so slightly out of view, and if I'm conspicuous on such a landscape, like the solitary figure of a woman I've just met with a baby on her back and two dogs moving swiftly as if across a sand-dune, she also inconspicuously vanishes. To say this magic place is haunted may be an exaggeration, but it feels a little like that.

And if Black Robin had his black horse, I have my black dog. What a companion. Not just because he doesn't answer back, because he does in a way, but because we're saved from the complex possibilities for communication that humans have but don't use very well. Just basics for Dog and I of love and survival. Several times he's sensed something in the woods beside a field astride the Down, as if it were a threat to our safety, and several times I've been relieved when he's turned away. No danger after all.

Poor Robin's horse, the story went, stopped eating when Robin hung on the gallows at Barham Cross Road. My conscience might not be snowy white but I've not robbed anyone recently, and if it were it to come to that, Dog isn't a big eater, so fasting wouldn't be too big a sacrifice.

Lydden Valley

Grass Dunes on down Downs

The word 'down' comes from the old English 'dun' meaning hill. Downs on the whole are ‘up', protruding in coombes and spurs, but the ones along the Lydden Valley are truly down. Approaching them from the wide plateau north east of Hawkinge just beside Everden farmhouse, they can be found plunging down as you walk out across the plateau. They are the down Down grass dunes of the dry valleys as opposed to the up ones of Arpinge and Etchinghill. But once you’ve descended into them you look up without it really being apparent that their tops only reach to the height of the base of another down.

Grass Dunes

Perusing the map before this walk I am chuffed to be reminded that my favourite valleys within the Circle form the acronym ELA. Elham Valley, Lydden Valley and Alkham Valley. Today before visiting the Lydden Valley’s softly striking curves I have already pulled myself out of a despond.

Like ELA, or Ella. She. Does. And has. An alternative.

But the despond in the middle of the night had seen the horror of a world bursting out, or was it falling through - cracks that could never be sealed, preventing sleep. Macbeth had murdered it and the tortured, sighing psyche of the universe heaved. The distant but continuous hum of some machine - was it underground, overhead or on the road? – had whirred on without ceasing. There is Seasonal Affective Disorder but I had woken up more than sad.

Over four years ago I'd started this walking, sad again, not to have my old walking companion to share the wonders seen. Then I got Dog. Now there is no despond in solitary walking, on the contrary. If SAD is a natural part of our makeup and we are about to descend into winter, it can also be counteracted despite the season. Merely the thought of this 'resource', or an image of these hills and beautiful valleys of Elham, Lydden and Alkham that form Ela, would, even if I was in prison, provide inner resolve and resuscitation. So much the better if I can get out there. It will further change me, and Dog is looking forward.

Before us lie qualities of the Garden of Eden. The lush grass so green it takes the breath away and so thick I'd feel padded enough to roll and fall into it. Delicious but subtle is the odour of damp I'm taken into as if into a gentle, moist autumn trance, trees ablaze in the distance way behind this luscious green.

We will take the route that we did one winter when the shadows of the bare trees were sharp, dark and long. But I can't open the gate and it's too high for Dog to jump so we're taken back into the valley of curves, which is what we came for, as if into ourselves.

I remember how I pursued sand-dunes on the edge of a Morrocan desert once. They are here right now as sheep-grazed 'grass dunes' in a late autumn English sun, one Sunday before the clocks go back.

Cloud Down

If yesterday our free way was marred by cows at Etchinghill, today sheep are dotted over the grass near Everden cottage, and again our cavorting is impeded. The bright sun that enticed me out is now smothered by an obstinate black cloud, persistent and pertinent in an otherwise blue sky. The covered orb's rays splay and gag out from its sides.

Despite the disappointment of this restriction we make our way over the grass dunes, down and up the other side towards Boyington Court where a raucous cacophony of unwelcoming dogs bark from two or three corners making us feel uneasy and keen to retreat asap. So we find a new route to return us to our original way through woods and follow it back to the grass dunes.

And now the sun is out.

As if by happenstance.

Not that the sun rises and sets but that it finds its way out from behind a murky charcoal cloud.

Shining blindingly in deep and curving tractor furrows.

A last blast that cuts through the Downs' flanks lighting up every blade of grass.

No wonder I dream of golden, shimmering, shining elf people sitting on a semi-circular edge of a pond as big as the sea, tending the ancient fire!

Dunes and Desert, Searingly Hot

The seasons are another country. I could have travelled a thousand miles as to Morroco to have got here, to them. This, the same place, is different, a different season a different place.

I am home but it has changed. And keeps on changing. Not just four times a year. It moves on in concentric circles moving outwards, then inwards, then outwards again. The land formation besides Everden Cottage that I've have seen many times, in many seasons, is new and different again. The familiar unfamiliar. The unfamiliar familiar. I didn't know that in coming to explore this ring, I would be coming to explore difference. All the differences in the same place. All the same place in the differences. I am elated.

It is searingly hot. It could be Greece as well as Morroco. Dog flies from shadow to shadow under trees but they are few and far between. As much as there was treacherous mud there are now treacherous grasses. We are compelled to explore because the clusters are so beautiful when green, and also now when bleached and dry.

Man

Whereas the cows at Etchinghill drove us out into a mandala, the sheep in the grass dunes near Everden Cottage are points we manoeuvre through, not around. Like yesterday, the day starts sunny and any clouds will go, says the forecast, like they did yesterday, so with sun in the offing I'm compelled to catch those grass dunes in it again.

Of course, there is no sun and it gets darker as we come at the dunes from a different angle, Foxhole, just outside Denton on the other side of Reinden Woods. But it's lovely to plummet down a bank into a picture I took when first coming across Lydden Valley some three years ago in winter, seeing it leafy now hanging in there despite autumn.

And a delight to discover this wild, unkempt part of the green valley we walk through, green, soft totts not ankle-twisting, carpeting the way. Until a man in grey green garb in a tiny open jeep, not much bigger than a drivable lawnmower approaches us frightening Dog with the roar of his engine, to point out I can't walk up there or along there, or down there, but must go back to stick on the marked footpath I've strayed from. Dog, I'd said to him isn't a problem with sheep, I'd keep him on the lead anyway, and he looks at me like he knows I know he thinks I'm lying. His dogs are running around somewhere at the top of the hill, chasing rabbits, he says. They won't hurt your dog if he's on the lead, he implies, but I look at him like I know he knows he's lying. One dog on the lead and another free,can be a recipe for disaster. Sure enough, his dog is all snarls and hackles-up, so he has to takes off to distract him from Dog.

His little engine rumbles noisily up the hill, down, across and up again while we make our way back, hearing more angry dogs bark and a shot now and again which I imagine must be the rabbits his dog has caught.

The lonely encounter with this man on a grey day was eerie and is perhaps why the empty landscape seems eerie too, seemingly absent with the people you know are there sometimes watching you.

Poor un-rich bitch that I am on someone else's land, perhaps I should have been more conciliatory. Our businesses here are as divided as different planets.

Mandalas are to do with goodwill and conviction in goodness. Fair weather things. If I believe there's a mandala, wholeness, I'm kidding myself, I think after this semi-skirmish, so frail is my sense of worth when threatened and my sense of place – I'm not entitled to be here – called to task.

Rainbow towards Lydden

From a path out of Alkham Valley in Ewell Minis, we descend through a wood we've retreated to from the stormy coast, in wind and rain. We push in to shelter under a bush, then emerge into a rainbow, crunching over acorns and autumn leaves to an open sunny valley. Instead of walking through it, we bear left and ascend and skirting around Brown's Woods to its edge in full sunshine, winding through Cold Blow, no mistake, bouncinge down once more and back through this golden valley, evening shadows descending with us behind Brown's Woods into Lord's.

Alkham Valley

Alkham: *'For the most part it is a quiet land of wood and coombes, of sudden winding valleys, lonely farms and solitary churches, everywhere laced with an intricate network of narrow lanes, steep hills and shady holloways, peaceful, silent and in many parts remote.'*

Alan Everitt *Continuity and Colonization 1986*

In the great sweeps and folds of Alkham's landscape, where geology is intrinsic, you can almost imagine the same riverine force of melting glaciers and movement that created the Alps millions of years ago, creating them.

Alkham comes from the Old English world *ealh* meaning temple (Branston, Brian, *The Lost Gods of England,* Thames and Hudson 1974 (First Edition 1957)

An Alkham April

A bright day after a miserable bout of flu. In need of a walk that's short, sharp and to the point, just enough but not too much to rekindle energy and imagination. A steep but not too long ascent up a tiny lane through habitations (did they have roses growing round their carved wooden doors?), dogs barking at Dog and a track onto an open, sharply sloping hill that looks out over everything. Other hills that slant down obliquely, falling in not opening out, to valleys transgressed by further spurs, over-crowdedly concentrating towards something. But what? Does the intricate valley form a kind of star shape?

While the scattered buildings of the village are almost incidental, a precisely curving mound on the other side of one valley, furrowed with deep plough marks, black in the bright sun's incisive shadow, again precisely placed with equal spaces between, seems to tilt forward, and a white horse balances on the edge of another field. Trees blossom in the churchyard. Other bosky patches allude to crevices that can't quite be interpreted from this height and Dog gets wind of rabbit. I throw a stick that sends him another way.

Onto a track, through a thicket and more tumble-down houses, that turns sharply away from the view over the valley. We're 'plateaued' till we reach another path that stretches across a field through a wood along the side of a hill with a swollen girth, enticing us up across stretching shadows to look down again at the village – before realising the path we need actually follows its base, where lies the stile.

This track takes us back along the deep valley to the one we started on. A sweet melody greets us. It's April, not the first time this year I've heard the sound of the blackbird's spring song that evokes memories older than memory. Deeper than a deep childhood remembrance of summer evenings and a crepuscular light streaming through birches outside my window into the very carpet of my floor – or later of a lover who's with me no more. A memory going too deep into time for loneliness. Deeper than me or mine. To a second without words of a joy deeper than time.

St Radigund's Abbey

Left and right and left and right again. Past Mount Ararat. At a slight bend to the right, I park the car to the side of the road and plunge down through a sunken track, probably a holloway, with a deep waterless gulley thick with golden brown beech leaves and flint stones.

The damp, composting ground and bare trees dripping with vapoury air feel perfect for the bright, jungle fresh green of Hart's-tongue fern, but a storm must recently have struck here for many tree trunks woven with ivy lie strewn over the path. Although it's silent and lovely, I have a job keeping upright on the slippery mud track as we come to the edge of the wood which opens out onto the slopes of the beautiful Alkham Valley.

I'm preoccupied with the map. Dog is getting bored while I try to work out how long we must keep going along this path bordering the field and wood, then how far down, up, across and up again? But already I'm foiled. How will we get to the other side of this tightly boarded by barbed-wired fence?

Then I see Dog behind another fence. He's found the path.

This is quickly becoming his walk, for to get around the fence by going back a little is to be on our allotted track within this liminal space between field and wood. So I tell him how clever he is to find our route, androute and, pleased with this, he returns to me so I can follow him as he shows me how to get onto the path too.

Yet, still busily consulting the map, I'm not fully appreciating my surroundings as we progress along the path between nasty scratching brushes and I'm am feeling reluctant about the whole business of descent and re-ascent across the valley. Dog finds another opening to our right instead of going left and down, and it doesn't take me long to accept his decision to strike upwards through Gorsehill and Stoneyhill woods, ancient oak woodlands from at least 1,600 BC. This takes the pressure off looking at the map continuously. We won't go so far now, besides this wood suddenly transforms to reveal its magical world of bark and branch, and more thick carpets of beech leaf as well as human half-habitation constructions logging up against tree trunks.

Mesmerised by the thick leaves as they swirl off the forest floor, with Dog careering and sliding after sticks, we keep going through the woods until we arrive at another ancient place, the remains of St. Radigund's Abbey, built in 1191 and occupied by monks from Premontre in France. In 1302, Edward I1 apparently received the great seal at St. Radigunds and delivered it to his chancellor, William Greenfield, but not much more is known of its history except that in 1538, along with other monasteries, it was suppressed. We're looking straight at its tower, or gatehouse, and behind it is a nave, transept, chapter house, cellarer's building and refectory. Wouldn't have found this if we'd followed my route rather than Dog's.

Walking at a right angle across a field, we're back at the car, but before getting in, we follow the initial path in its circuitous opposite other direction just for a bit until I recognise the woods I've often come through leading up from Alkham.

It's good to be playing with footpaths, not map-bound, following them through the woods until it gets dark. Unmapped I'm elated. But also alone. That in itself – probably just meaning that nobody can do for me what being out here can right now – isn't bad. Just the negative offshoot thoughts of that that come rolling up on a cold wind as betrayals, dis-entwinings and disapppointments. Terrors even that make us rein ourselves in and clip our wings.

Didn't want to mar the day, and maybe these dismal thoughts have a cathartic function, but suddenly Dog, as if also aware of the 'slings and arrows', is standing distressed in the middle of a field where he'd gone to retrieve the stick I'd thrown. He is not moving but attacking his fur. I recognise the signs of burr intrusion, his retaliating reflexes the opposite to self-harm. Large ones have burrowed deep into his fur and enmeshed under leg-pits, elbows and throat, sitting close to his skin. You, who've shown me the path today, aren't alone, I say kneeling in the mud and stubble to take out what I can, while he continues pulling out fragments of burr along with fur till they fall to the ground. As there's no sign of burr bushes nearby, these must be from the broken off scattered branches. When we get home, I explain, we'll get out the comb to free you of this pernicious pricked-ness in no time at all.

And, still from these woods, I'll have taken back more thoughts than I brought. Of lovers and loved ones in their place, friendships not destroyed or subsumed by this nature we enter but dying down. Sprouting up. From earth and shrub and tree. In grass and flower and leaf.

St Radigund's

It is over a year since we were here and now again the path is beset with treachery, brambles that tear my legs and rain jacket, pulling off my woolly hat. But we've come too far to retreat. However, when a tree with many a spreading branch strewn across the path proves too difficult to get over, under or around, I'm defeated.

A shape which is Dog moves off to my right, now he is standing there, my guiding spirit beckoning for me to follow. This is the way. There is no getting back to the path, the scrub is too thick and thorny. Each time I clamber and fall up through the soft leaves of the forest that we must now transverse upwards, he is standing waiting, making sure I am doing ok. It is tough going upwards, I feel the ache in my thighs from different muscles put to work, not to mention the scratches from brambles all over my legs which I can feel but not see, and the next morning I discover my coordinated green checked Next trousers are completely ruined, lacerations appearing in white stitch from the green checks.

Eventually we come to the path that we should have reached turning off the other one.

This was the walk Dog found the path for last time.

And, when we get to Radigund's, it is in full sunshine this time.

Radegund, born in 518 AD, was a Thuringian princess and Frankish queen, i.e. daughter of the pagan king of Thurigia in Southern Germany, who was taken prisoner by the invading Frank King at about the age of ten and later became the notorious womaniser's wife. Though beautiful, she was very pious, wearing a shift of haircloth with iron chains and collars, and hot plates of iron under her robes, abstaining from eating flesh, fish, eggs or fruit. When Clothier had her brother murdered, she went to Poitiers and became deaconess of a religious house. The Bishop of Paris persuaded her husband to leave her alone and in 557 she built the monastery of the Holy Cross, a centre of learning for monks and nuns, and the year later received a fragment of the true cross.

The Abbey dedicated to her was founded in 1191, taking fifty years to build, and a community was established by canons sent over from Premontre. By the thirteenth century, because the site was inhospitable, the monks were involved with building Dover Castle, and by the fourteenth it was falling into neglect. In the Dissolution of the Monasteries, much of its stone was carried away to build Sandgate Castle, but what is left still looks fully textured in the light of the setting sun.

Church Hougham

Unicorns

Perched on the backbone of a finger of hill rippling Dover-wards we set out from Church Hougham under a jet-black sky that edges its way towards us like a rain-filled roof. The exposed track is fenced to begin with so no way of retreating under trees if this roof cloud opens. Yet, glorious sunshine lies on the ground beneath our feet, spreading over the fields, sky and trees. The rain holds off as we walk beside a rainbow and find a strong sign attached to a gatereading, '*Beware of the Unicorn*'.

West Hougham: Huffing out

A square with shaky, almost round corners, almost a mandala, forms the streets of West Hougham. Where, I wonder is Hougham? Later I discover it to be exactly where we walked today. Naturally, I imagine it must be bigger than the civilised West Hougham, whose streets are marked skimpily by this square, but surprisingly, when I look on the map, I find Hougham to be devoid of habitation, i.e. it is marked somewhere near the middle of a field near Long Wood and the reeded 'sole' (old word for pond.)

A hollowness is what inadvertently comes to me in Hougham, pronounced Hoffam or Huffam, and I huff and puff and blow it all out. I have brought my own emptiness to this lovely high space looking over valleys to more wooded hills and right through to Dover Caste sitting on the horizon above the sea. What coincidence that the bigger area marked on the map is not a city or a town or a village but earth and tree and grass, the mandala square village beside it.

Devoid of the need for people, though not lonely or without feeling, I wonder have I let others down, or they me? Still a strange almost unnerving feeling, hanging here, above the sea, not disappointed with my surround, insurround, in suspense rather than limbo, in awe of air that fills the soul while also waiting still for it to be filled again, and more.

Perhaps that's what this mandala,the squared circle of West Hougham, is to me. Freedom from people and the disquiet they cause, twinned with the sustenance they can no longer offer. *A Town called Paradise* by Van Morrison plays from my CD in the car and I save some of its words for myself.

New Paths

In the summer the paths are more in-path-able than in muddy winter. They have disappeared altogether, nettles, brambles, thistles grow up, not just from their banks but lean perniciously right across their route. The passable path-able paths now criss-cross fields of barley and corn, we can follow them where we will, willy-nilly, just round the field itself, especially when to crawl off to their sides involves more nettles and thistles leading in the case of Hougham to a nice valley, yes, but two horses, little and large, who, after a fox retreats, stampede down the grass avenue towards us. We would have taken this route had not a couple of donkeys turned up too. Dog and the donkeys lock into a confront-and-run game, Dog unaware that they might buck and kick their back legs out at him, so we turn round, go back to the zig-zag paths that cut narrowly and deeply through the heavy summer crop.

Farthing Common and West Wood

Stone Street is the Roman route that slices through the centre of the North Downs. From Farthing Common, we follow it for a while before descending into Stowting and out again on an ancient track to criss-cross back over it, skirting the southern edge of West Wood, back through Hempstead and Skeete, and round the back of the garden centre.

Our Father Who Art in Nature

High on the Downs and into the interior behind Farthing Common in October 2016, Dog and I walk the yellow and black signed Public Footpath. On telegraph poles I notice other yellow and black signs saying '*Danger of Death*'. Yellow is two-fold and so is something about a dead fox that we come across lying on the grass, its face and ears almost whole but the fur on its body sinking into the earth as if it were just another part of the grass growing there.

An idea came to me about how to explain the opposite of Descartes' *I think therefore I am* that causes Dualism, the separation of thinker from object, person from land, mind from body, God from man. It is like the form of the word Pan-theism, meaning god (theism) in everything (pan), no distinction between the divine and the human. A pantheist believes that all nature is made of God. So does philosophical alchemy.

Leaving the fields we walk a path in West Wood, a straight path, I feel, a repetitive thing, until like entering the liminal world of seashore at low-tide the lines marking its edges melted and dissolveed away like entering the liminal world of seashore at low-tide. I'm in another zone like with the seashore. But now to levels and layers of leaf, bark, branch and trunk of pine, beech, birch and fir. Deeply textured, deeply receding. Foliage of thistle and bracken and autumn orange. Odours of sap, damp, mud, decomposing leaves and gulch.

A carpet of golden-brown leaves of beech off the track leads into a dark glade of firs, black leaf, black trunk, almost black as non-light night in between, yet the golden-brown leaves, threading between dark and light, lead into another glade of bright: each spring-green birch leaf interspersed with light on this early afternoon full with elevation.

Piercing between distant, further trees the sun has pinched itself into a cold, tight ball, and the fresh, green leaves, which could have belonged to spring instead, are tinged, as if in compensation for this dark illusion, with saffron and crimson. It's then, knowing even as we slip back into a dualism that can be dissolved Pan-theistic style, that we find our way out from the levels and layers, back onto the lined path.

Bluebell Woods

Pillars Woods, April 2017

At the edge of the eye, a dusty grey come cornflower blue. Looking full on a luscious carpet of blue seeping into a wooded distance, not much spring green yet just bracken, and Dog and I just walking, following one track after another until we reach a particular one I recognise.

Here, two years ago, a particular, peak experience – pure wonder of Dog and I in it – a twisting path, a bankside bluebell carpet, some dwindling anenomes dotted around, ramsons awaiting arrival.

And now my remembrance of that as a feeling. A moment not limited to that moment, and while I repeat the pictures of Dog, I repeat the feeling, repeating it differently now. Beginning anew again.

The carpet of bluebell suddenly seems divided into soft cornflower rectangles of life, I wandering without thinking. Without a map. Liable to get lost. Rectangles of life and I always walking the paths through them, choosing a route. In these woods – and this doesn't matter – they all lead, carpet upon carpet of blue, one into another. No choice to be made. No success or failure. This is the magic. Dog remembers and poses for me.

March 2018

I am looking for dryness under the rain, for light under the cloud. The weather forecast says there'll be a break between four and six o'clock, so we leave the coast to head for the hills, but the fog descends around us thicker than the rain. The drifts of snow have melted and sunk into the forest floor. The rain adds to the squelch and the peaty puddles and the leaves on the forest floor, a sponge of sodden leaves sinking and rising underfoot, are a bouncy mulch, and the leafless trees, many fallen and flowing along the ground, are bleak but bend into a bountiful brown.

Although it's still wintry, this is March not November, winter's end not beginning, this thick squelch and drip providing succour for the riches of bluebell and ramson flora to come.

We walk along the edge of the wood in a field the other side of a fence. This is where Dog has demanded I throw sticks. But there are no breaks in the fence which leads us around two sides of a square, so we follow it back. More solid tracks than the mulch lead us to our parking, but not before I've glimpsed four small Gurkha soldiers crossing behind us without acknowledgement in silent stealth, which leaves my heart shaking a bit and pleased to close the car door and drive away.

Back to the coast through the fog which suddenly evaporates under a brightness from the sea and is just as quickly replaced by new mist in this huge amphitheatre of edgeness – Pillar Woods near Paddlesworth sits at a high point on the Downs – and homeward under a ceiling of cloud and rain. For a short while, the fog over the sea is held captivated in a self-contained disk, lit from underneath before spilling out of itself into an amorphous light-stealing expanse.

From Long Wood, near Brabourne

Knowing mostly which hill is which in this topography, like places on my body, I'm heading to one where I know there are woods just above Brabourne. No sooner seeing a tree line ascending up its side, I'm within it, a holloway track leading up in protected safety from the roaring wind that sounds like a monster trying to break through, loose flint and chalk holding us.

Today, May 1st, 2017, is chill enough for hail. From a deep dell to a bluebell, I skirt around myself. Was it really a year since we last did this, and what is this path I've not been on before leadings through a fairy tale and round to to the entrance we entered, looking out over this vista?

~ 6 ~

THE SAXON SHOREWAY

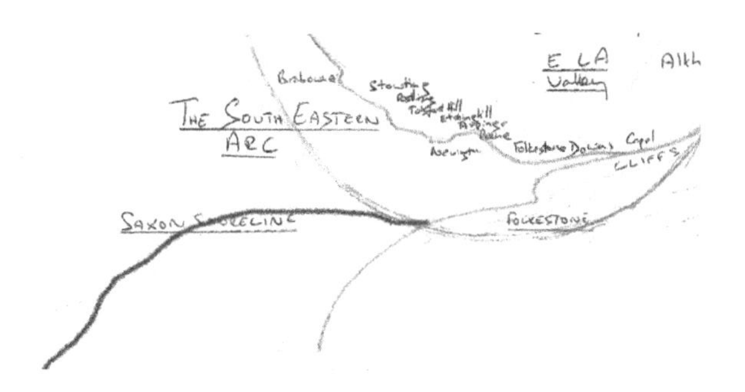

The Saxon Shoreway is a long-distance path that traces the south-east coast as it was in Roman times, from Gravesend to Hastings. What is now Romney Marshes was once a sea-bed and what is now the Royal Military Canal was once the River Rother flowing near the base of cliffs. It is a significant landmass within sight our North Downs's Ring.

Saxon Shoreline overlooking Hythe

Edge Place I

When I'm walking through golden grass on the slopes of the Saxon shore-lineshoreline am I scaling the incline of an ancient white cliff or am I closer to the yellow sand of a beach?

At the liminal canal-filled base of these slopes, a heron emerges and wings its way over the tumbling down grasses. A dragon-fly hovers and flitters away. Some things mark us, I'm reminded of what a friend said, and, although she means bad things, there are also the good.

A river once flowed along the watery liminality of the Saxon shoreline now occupied by a canal. Water moves inexorably. It is possible that four things have marked me. A death. Another death. A madness. An abandonment. It's possible there are more and these are only the tip of the iceberg we left in these places, always between one thing and another. For there are also the sweet things. The bearing of children. The discovery of lovers. The effortless fluency of water. Today in the trees around the canal that was once a river a breeze of eternal change sounds into the liminal golden-grassed place's absolute quiet.

Edge Place II

Where it not for the long, strong, honey-coloured grasses of these clusters of hillocks, I'd think we were in sand dunes again, but Dog and I are gambolling across the Roughs on a December late afternoon. Everything, whether reedy grass or sand is due to turn more golden, then pinky-peach, before the sun goes altogether over once faulting fault lines exacerbated by erosion.

So here we are on the Saxon shoreline, romping on what was perhaps previously sea, wondering if the seawater would have covered these grassy hillocks, wondering when was the Saxon shoreline a shoreline, when would we have been standing or swimming in sea looking up at cliffs? But there's no exposed chalk on these grassy escarpments. In fact, they look more like Downs.

We take a zigzag up towards the summit along narrow muddy animal paths, the pale honeycomb grasses shining, the surface they create spongy and ankle twisting. There are several little plateaux before we get to the summit path on the edge of a massive field that traverses each spur's zenith, following the top. It gets harder to keep a grip. Massive badger or fox holes cave in under foot and remnants of spikey iron railings stab at my feet, so I'm frightened of tripping and slipping. And what a drop.

But, with Dog in the lead, I totter along until there is no path and apparently no way of getting down to a strange concrete structure that looks like a huge horn. There is also dark rock, not chalk, on this very steep scarp. It seems there is no way down. But I don't want to go back, so sit and slide over the soft totts without falling and make it to the bottom.

Four Roman forts built in the fourth century to repel the Saxons were built along the Saxon shoreline in Reculver, Richborough, Dover and Lympne. But here we are beside a listening mirror, relic from WW1, detector of unwanted aircraft, and here is the official path down on shorter velvety grass.

The sun is shining more lately through the reedy grasses. Dog has found a stick that makes him dance. And while striding down-hill without concentrating now I'm off the treacherous cliffy edge, I do slip, splat, onto my back, winding myself through and through, shocking my torso. Dog just wants his stick. And, so, my momentary pain is gone. If I have aches and pains tomorrow, I will still relive how I was in this zone, straddling earth and water, weighted and weightless upon a subtly shifting littoral of squelchy marsh.

Rough Roughs

Suddenly, while trying to find a route away from the young and pernicious stinging nettles and rather exotic looking green and white dappled, also pernicious, thorn bushes, we lose the path altogether. Or at least, it is a tiny one made by sheep, and Dog follows at my heal knowing I can protect him a little from the stings and pricks. I wonder how much he feels. A dog's instinct to hide their vulnerability from would-be predators.Today the Roughs really do feel rough, but not to begin with as we climb jauntily towards the sound mirror summit. I remember how here on the Saxon Shoreline slopes the May blossom always seems thicker than elsewhere, or perhaps this is just where the little hawthorns like to be.

Approaching the sound mirror, the nettles don't thin at all. It's really unpleasant walking and although the views are fine, I'm stung and pricked through my trousers. Climbing over humpy-dumpy hills towards a greener summit, the nettles are almost blue with maliciousness, so we turn around for home.

But the totts of grass are ankle-breaking. I have to tread very slowly and carefully. Dog waits in anticipation but also looks for water in the lower marsh under the tree, near the canal. He can't reach it and so his quenching in the slightly unpleasant heat can only take place from his bowl back in the car. While the Roughs experience has left me a little wobbly, my remembering eyes are still filled, even the day after, with intense whiteness of May blossom and open vistas of the bay, and I float on its white liminal flower while the steady sap rises on these days that hover assuredly between spring and summer.

Saxon Shoreline overlooking Hythe

Through the Zoo

Late June 2017. Just past midsummer around the perimeters of the wildlife sanctuary.

Squaring the sloping hill we will go down, across, up and along.

The day is grey, sultry, dry, except for a damp veneer left from yesterday's rain that only lightly carpets the cracked, heavy earth.

At the beginning of the square, I am cool, at the end, caked in sweat.

Out of the damp, lush stillness after deluge, comes the peep, peep, peep of bird call like a drop of no longer falling rain.

Brown butterflies rising round the Roman fort.

Out of the damp, still air come a myriad of smells that invade Dog's quivering nostrils. African Wild Dogs on the other side of the fence.

Gentle giraffes that bow their heads.

The horses in the field with stripes, yes, zebras, are absent as we walk the last side of the square back to the car. And, yes, here on the Saxon shoreline where tigers, eastern bongos, greater kudus, common elands, painted dogs, tigers, rhinos, ostriches, wolves, giraffes and tapirs wander around as if they are in Africa or their natural habitat, you can cast your eyes over plains and sea to a truth stranger than fiction.

Ghosts

Heat, hay and haze accompany our search for the stream which we only find at the end, for the golden field burgeoning with crop keeps us in its bends, not circles, and directs us away from the path leading to the water on this plateau, on the other side of the road to the zoo. Like on the last walk, I start off almost chilly, wondering if I should have brought a jacket, but as our rhythm quickens through these grooves of wheat and the sun burns, just a little through the haze, I'm getting hot and Dog is panting and rushing to find some shade of which there is none.

We are on a ledge now too far away from the water in the valley. The fields are too heavily in growth to be walked across so we sit by a patch of wild flowers to eat egg and cress sandwiches. Then, when we are almost back, I see what must be the track we should have taken to get to the water, so we descend it now and dog wriggles his way through more thick brambles, grasses, crops and big leaves to quench his thirst in a trickle of a stream, so small but welcomed as in any parched desert.

The golden crop is wholesome but heavy, full from the sultry air which has bred it, a dusty but swelling ripeness in this land of plenty.

From this plateau that's burgeoning with heat, wheat and dust, not lush – that one's in a green-crop field below beyond brambles we cannot cross – I can see out to the North Downs. But, as I'm on the ridge of a plain between the cliff rising over the Saxon shoreline and the Downs, I'm further down from the usual recognisable landmarks of Brockman Bushes or Tolsford Hill and this range is new to me.

From this plateau I feel elated. My solitariness is all. But is it? What of this emptiness that hurlings itself at me? Could it be in the deep recollection of countryside that was once a busy place, jostling with villagers and scythes, the waggon full with harvest, the stacked wheat sheaves, the queen of the harvest riding high. With this in mind, it is a strange place indeed. Empty. Still. Lifeless apart from the crop and the ghosts of people departed.

Un-straight-jacketed

(Beach before Dymchurch)

Wondrous thing to be able to walk out on the straight of a concrete line and return along the curve of the tide.

Decked stairs run down through the rocks into the sea when we set out along the raised concrete walk, high tide lapping up against the base of boulders stopping us getting to the beach. Yet, at each path Dog and I played down, the more the sand appeared at the bottom, until by the time we turned, the tide was turning too, more noticeably, to reveal sand and more sand slithered over by a shallow dying wave spreading silkily out over it with white edgings of frilly fans.

Spreading but withdrawing, peeling back and back.

Bliss.

Between a rock and a soft sea place, we run and play in and out of the waves, no longer straight-jacketed by the straight and narrow walk on the wall.

Romney Marshes

Walland Marsh

~ 7 ~

CONCLUSION

Finding a mandala pattern for ourselves in the outside world before us or under our feet, whether it be in stupa, chapel, intersection of cabbage, half-apple or daisy, is to reflect something of the possibility of our own mandala of inner wholeness, Jung's 'individuation', derived from the matter we have often dismissed as of lesser value than our strivings purely 'upwards'.Nature as 'matter 'has long been associated with the feminine and, as such, relegated by patriarchy to a level inferior to that of the masculine 'spirit'. Our journey to seek out the mandala of place in nature is to contest this attitude and try to repair some of the damage we see it has caused to nature and women. To cherish what we have on our doorsteps is to encourage us to nurture our natural world. The Latin word *mater* not only means mother but also source and origin. The loss of connection with these beginnings corresponds to the loss of a sense of the 'sacred feminine' in nature, now an urgent issue.

Mandala in Sanskrit means 'the circle' and can be further translated, as 'the place that holds or contains the ultimate essence'. From 'poisons' to the wisdoms of the Mandala of the Five Dakinis (Tsultrim Allione's *Wisdom Rising*), it provides a map for returning to the ground of our being. Mandalas reflect the structure of the universe from the smallest microcosm to the vastest macrocosm. They are birth places. Sacred enclosures or places for spiritual rituals or practices. Even the world in its ever-present chaos could be viewed as an ever-evolving mandala.

So, if I've been seeking, on these Downs, to become a Tibetan-styled *dakini,dakini,*' a 'sky dancer', 'she who moves through space', so be it. I hope others will join me. Our 'upwards' lie in our 'downwards'. And with my trusty Dog, onto whom I've projected a little of my own spirit as the embodiment of imaginative thought, I seek out the mandala unself, myself coming out of myself, ready to meet the shape and breath and light of what spills from nature's hill and flatland and flower.